THE MEANEST MAN IN THE ARMY

and Other Stories of Grace

Also by Stuart Tyner:
Chosen by Grace
Grace Notes
Searching for the God of Grace
The Colors of Grace in Our Homes

Illustrated by
Alexander Skibelski

THE MEANEST MAN IN THE ARMY

and Other Stories of Grace

Written by
Stuart Tyner

REVIEW AND HERALD® PUBLISHING ASSOCIATION
Since 1861 | www.reviewandherald.com

Published by Review and Herald® Publishing Association, Hagerstown, MD 21741-1119

Review and Herald® titles may be purchased in bulk for educational, business, fund-raising, or sales promotional use. For information, e-mail SpecialMarkets@reviewandherald.com.

The Review and Herald® Publishing Association publishes biblically based materials for spiritual, physical, and mental growth and Christian discipleship.

This book was
Edited by Penny Estes Wheeler and Rachel Cabose
Copyedited by Delma Miller
Designed by Emily Ford / Review and Herald® Design Center
Cover illustration by Alexander Skibelski
Interior illustrations by Alexander Skibelski
Typeset: Minion Pro 12.5/15

PRINTED IN U.S.A.

18 17 16 15 14 5 4 3 2 1

Library of Congress Cataloging-in-Publication Data
Tyner, Stuart, 1946-
The meanest man in the Army : and other stories of grace / Stuart Tyner.
pages cm
Includes index.
ISBN 978-0-8280-2729-8
1. Bible stories, English. 2. Bible—Biography—Juvenile literature. 3. Grace (Theology)—Juvenile literature. 4. Seventh-Day Adventists—Doctrines—Juvenile literature. I. Title.
BS551.3.T96 2014
221.9'505—dc23
2013015349

ISBN 978-0-8280-2729-8

These stories of grace are for

Emma and Sophie,

Jacob and Joshua,

Gabriel and Lyra.

"Grandparents are proud of their grandchildren."

—Proverbs 17:6, CEV.

Contents

About the Author

Popular author Stuart Tyner
has spent a lifetime teaching, preaching,
and writing about his favorite subject:
God's incredible grace.

More than anything,
he wants children to know the profound,
motivating truth that "Jesus loves me."
Recently retired from pastoring,
Tyner lives in Riverside, California,
with his wife, Karen. They have three
adult children and six grandchildren.

Preface for Parents

Imagine a young child climbing up on her mother's lap and saying, "Read me a story, please." What Bible-based resource will the mother choose?

Imagine a bedtime scene with two small children, teeth brushed, toys put away, tucked into bed by their parents, who now want to provide a few minutes of family worship before the kids go to sleep. Where will they turn for a biblically sound, spiritually appropriate short story to read?

Consider grandparents on a summer Friday evening with their grandchildren visiting. What book will they open to share their love of Jesus with their young family?

And think about a single mom, wanting to provide spiritual nourishment for her child. What Bible story book will she read that will capture the child's interest and lay a deep spiritual foundation?

Parents and grandparents of preschool- and school-age children frequently ask these questions. They want to create a friendly atmosphere for nurturing a personal relationship with Jesus. They want their children to begin their lives with a biblically well-founded understanding of the riches, kindness, forbearance, and patience of God (Romans 2:4). They want their children to love God and not be afraid of Him (1 John 4:18). They want the gospel to "bear fruit" and grow in their children's experience (Colossians 1:6). They desire that their children anticipate the promised Second Coming while not fearing it (2 Peter 3:13). A parent recently related to me the prayer of her 5-year-old: "Please, please, please, please make heaven come quickly!" That's what many parents hope for their children.

The Bible contains more than 400 stories. Not all of them are appropriate for young children. Not every story meets a child where he or she is and builds the confidence of a warm relationship with God. Some stories will have to wait for more maturity and explanation. But there are stories of people helping others, serving as Christ did. There are stories about growing up in the family of God, learning the power of their traditions, absorbing the Christ-centered culture, learning how and why to obey all of God's commands. There are stories about God's people worshipping Him with all their hearts and souls and minds.

We begin here with the foundation: stories of God's goodness to us, stories of grace. A simple reading through Genesis to Revelation may at times confuse even the most grounded adults. So with children in the faith we chose stories from the Old Testament and the New Testament that testify of Jesus. And like Jesus on the road to Emmaus (Luke 24:27), we explain what the stories have to teach us about our Master.

To capture and hold the interest of our children, these stories are short and simple, even predictable. God is revealed as our friend and companion, a parent who desires our best. He walks with us, talks to us, explains things, and generously promises never to leave us. The pictures paint the portrait of God with loving brushstrokes. We want the children to peer into the pages their parents are reading to them and ask questions about the stories and the pictures that depict the actions they are listening to.

There's also a little extra in each chapter for you. Background material helps us understand the stories even better, and additional biblical support is available for parents to read in their own devotional time. This deeper theological encouragement comes from appreciating how these priceless stories reveal God's love, goodness, patience, and kindness—the unending, amazing grace of God. You'll find these additional materials at the close of every chapter in the section titled Endnotes for Parents.

I've chosen 15 Old Testament stories for this first volume, and 15 more for a New Testament book. There are memory verses for each story, passages that kids can memorize and repeat later.

It is my prayer that the retelling of these simple Bible stories will strike a responsive note in the hearts and minds of Adventist families everywhere and provide a welcome resource for parents to read with their children.

Strangers on Earth

Before we start reading the stories in this book, let's play a few pretend games together, OK? (You can play all these games today and then read the stories later. Or you can play just one game before you read a story, and then play another game before the next time you read a story. Whatever you choose.) Are you ready? Here we go.

Pretend Game 1

Let's pretend we need to go to the grocery store together. There are lots of items on our list to buy. (What would you like to get at the store? I'm in the mood for a big, juicy Fuji apple! What do you want?)

We get our cart and go up and down the aisles. We take items from this side and that and put them in the cart. When we're all through shopping, we go to the front of the store and get in line. The checker takes each item, rings it up on her register, and then gives us the bill. The rule at the grocery store is that first you pay the bill, and then you get to take the groceries home. That's the way things work in our world, isn't it?

Now, pretend the checker greets you with a big surprise. "We have a treat for you today," she says with a happy smile on her face. "Somebody who loves you very much has already paid for your groceries! You get to take home everything in your cart. And you don't have to pay a penny!" That would be a surprise, wouldn't it? A really happy surprise. We'd jump up and down and be very thankful. All the way home we'd have big smiles on our faces. And we couldn't wait to tell everybody about the nice thing that happened to us at the grocery store.

Pretend Game 2

Let's pretend you have already started school. I'm sure you're a very good student. (What subject will be your favorite? I always liked my history classes best. What will you enjoy studying?)

You listen to your teacher every day. You do all your homework. And you answer all the questions on the tests you take. You want to graduate to the next level in school with excellent grades. But the rule at this school is that you have to pass all your classes with absolutely no mistakes, and only then do you get to move to the next grade. That's the way things work in this school. It's tough, but that's the rule.

Now, pretend your teacher comes to you one day with your report card. You've been worried about this day for a long time, because you know you've made some mistakes. But your teacher is smiling. He says, "I've decided to treat you just as if you've always passed every test with a perfect score and done all your homework without making any mistakes! You get to graduate." That would be a lovely thing for your teacher to do, wouldn't it? You'd like that teacher very much, I'm guessing. Graduation day would be one of the happiest days in your life.

Pretend Game 3

Let's pretend we're planning to take a big vacation together. We can go anywhere in the world we want to go. (Where would you like to travel? I think I want to go to Paris, France. What place would you choose?)

We make all the arrangements. We check the weather in the place to which we are traveling. We pack our suitcases. We get in the car and head to the airport. We take our suitcases up to the counter and give the agent our tickets. But before the agent lets us board the plane, she insists that we show her our passports. The rule at the airport is there's no traveling out of the country without a passport. "Sorry if this ruins your vacation plans," the agent says, "but that's the way it works at the airport."

Now, imagine that the agent takes one more look at your tickets. "Oh, excuse me," the agent says. "I didn't notice this note. The person who paid for your tickets also left his passport to give to you. You can fly to your destination because his passport is good for you. You're free to go right ahead and board the plane." What a happy trip that would be! We'd have the best vacation ever! And we couldn't wait to tell everyone about what a wonderful gift someone left for us at the airport.

Pretend Game 4

Let's pretend it's your birthday and we're going to have a big party for you. All of your friends are invited. And we're making your favorite birthday cake. (What flavor do you want it to be? I'd say chocolate. What would you choose?)

Everybody at the party is in good spirits. The cake is delicious! The games are really fun. Now it's time to open your birthday presents. Your friends have gone all out to give you special, expensive gifts. You open each one and tell your friends how happy their gifts have made you. Then you go to your room and get the little bank in which you've been saving pennies, nickels, dimes, and quarters. You return to your friends and say, "I want to pay you for the presents." And you give each friend a shiny nickel to pay for the gifts.

But your friends are confused. The rule at birthday parties is that you give gifts to the birthday person because you love them. You choose gifts to give that will make your friend happy. You don't sell the presents! Trying to pay for the presents breaks *the giving rule*. Now that you understand *the giving rule*, you take back your nickels and give your friends a big hug for their sweet gifts.

Pretend Game 5

Let's pretend that in the middle of your birthday party you suddenly start to feel bad in your stomach. Maybe you had too much cake, you think. (Have you ever been really sick? What did it feel like?)

You feel worse and worse. Your parents rush you to the emergency room in the hospital. A doctor takes a close look at you and decides you need emergency surgery. Hours later you wake up in a hospital bed, the surgery complete. It takes several days for you to fully recover. The doctor comes to visit. "I'm ready to go home," you say to your doctor. But the doctor frowns. "The rule at this hospital is that you get to go home only after you've paid all your bills," the doctor tells you. "There is an emergency room bill. There's the emergency doctor's bill. There's the surgery bill. And the bill for all the nurses. And the bill for the hospital room. I'm sorry, but you can't go home until you pay every penny of the bill. That's the rule." You begin to wonder if you'll ever get home.

Then imagine that your doctor breaks into a big smile. "But I've got a surprise for you," the doctor says. "I'm so happy to have made you well again that I'm going to pay all your bills for you too. The emergency room, the doctors and nurses, the hospital room—I'm going to pay for them all! Your bill is fully paid. Now you can go home today." What a sweet thing for your doctor to do! We already love the doctor for taking such good care of you. Now we love the doctor even more for being so kind.

Living by God's Rules

In our world we live by the rules. "You can't take the groceries home until you pay for them." "You can't graduate until you pass every class." "You can't travel out of the country without a passport." "You don't sell birthday presents." "You can't go home from the hospital until all your bills are paid." And there are hundreds more rules. Everywhere we turn, more rules. The rules make sense for our world. We get along in life best when we follow all the rules.

In God's world there also are rules. But these rules are very different from the rules in our world. God's rules are full of wonderful surprises. God's rules are more like this: "Somebody who loves you very much has already paid for your groceries!" "I've decided to treat you just as if you've always passed every test with a perfect score and done all your homework without making any mistakes!" "The person who paid for your tickets also left his passport to give to you." "God gives gifts because He loves us and wants us to be happy. God doesn't sell His gifts to us." "God is so happy to have made us well, that He pays all our bills so we can go home too."

We call God's rules the Rules of Grace. When it comes to the great gift of living with Jesus in heaven for eternity, grace means God does for us what we can't do for ourselves. Grace means God pays the bill. Grace means God treats us just as if we'd never made a mistake. Grace means we travel to heaven on God's passport, not our own. We can't pay for His gift. It makes Him happy to do it for us.

And we thank Him by not being afraid of Him. We're happy to be near Him. We accept His gifts with joy. We love to tell other people about how good and kind and generous God is. We tell the stories of grace to everyone who will listen.

That's what the stories in this book are all about. They are stories of God treating us with grace. As you read every story, listen for the ways God treats us with the happy Rules of Grace. That will put a big smile on your face every day!

A. Skib

1

All Done!

"God saw all that he had made, and it was very good."

Genesis 1:31.

You and I have two places we call home. The first is the place where we live right now. Some of us live in a house, and some of us live in an apartment. Some of us live with two parents, and some of us live with just one. Some of us have brothers and sisters, and some of us are the only child our parents have.

But we also have another place we call home. I'm not talking about a summer home on a lake. Or a mountain cabin we visit on the weekends. Or a vacation house at the beach. Some of us may have several houses we call home, but I'm not talking about any of these.

I'm talking about a different home. It's in a place far, far away. And someday, when Jesus comes, we'll all go there together. We'll move into a beautiful new home that He has built just for us.

Let's talk about that other home in the place that's far, far away. It's a place our great-great-great-great-grandparents all heard about. It's a place we call heaven. But first, let's talk about the first home that Jesus made for the very first people: Adam and Eve.

Two Ways to Make a Home

There were two ways Jesus could have made a home for Adam and Eve.

One way was to make them do all the work. He could have said, "Adam and Eve, you're going to need a place to live, but don't worry; here's some wood and some paint. Over here is a bucket

of nails and plenty of electric wire. Right there is a two-week supply of food, and around the corner I've put a big barrel of water for you to drink from. But it will last just a few days, so you'd better get to work!"

A Better Way to Build a Home

Or Jesus could have done something very, very different. He could have done all the work Himself. He could have made sure everything was ready, then invited Adam and Eve to move in and enjoy the home He had made for them.

Which way do you think Jesus did it?

The Bible tells us exactly what happened. Jesus did all the work Himself.

First Jesus turned on the lights so Adam and Eve wouldn't have to live in the dark. Then He made the air fresh and clean so they could breathe freely and be healthy. Jesus put dry land around the water so Adam and Eve wouldn't get wet until they wanted to. He planted trees and plants in all the right places so Adam and Eve would have shade from the sun and good food to eat. He made sure that they would know when to go to sleep and when to wake up. He even put fish in the waters, birds in the sky, and animals in the fields and forests so Adam and Eve wouldn't be alone.*

A Very Special Place

Then Jesus created a very special place. He called it the Garden of Eden. It was the most beautiful place on the beautiful new earth. There was plenty of food on the trees and bushes. There were beautiful flowers. There was land and sea. There was night and day. In the sky during the day there was a big, bright, warm sun. At night there were a big, round moon and thousands of stars.

Adam and Eve would have time to explore every corner of the garden and to meet every one of the animals.

The work was all done. Everything was finished. Everything looked good and smelled good and tasted good. Everything was perfect. This beautiful home was ready for people to come live in it.

And *then* Jesus made Adam and Eve. When Adam and Eve opened their eyes for the very first time, they were already living in their new home.

Another New Home

The Garden of Eden reminds me of the new home that Jesus is making for *you* and for me. Jesus has put a lot of thought into making this home just right for us.

Jesus thought about the colors that would be our favorites. (What's your favorite color?)

Jesus thought about the tastes we'd enjoy the most. (What do you like to eat more than anything else in the world?)

And Jesus thought about the adventures that would make us most excited. (What's the most fun you've had this week?)

Jesus is setting up all those things for you and me. He's putting the good things in our new home so it will be ready for us when we get there. It will be perfect, just like the Garden of Eden was for Adam and Eve. We call our new home heaven.

Our Perfect Home Is Ready

We don't have to do the work to make heaven our home any more than Adam and Eve had to make their first home. Jesus does all the work. There's nothing more that needs to be done. The work is already finished. Our home in heaven is just waiting for us.

We won't have to work hard to figure out how to make it more interesting. It's already perfect just like it is.

We won't be bored or unhappy, because Jesus has filled heaven with all the things that make us the most happy.

We don't have to be afraid that we aren't good enough to live in heaven. Our heavenly home is ours because of the grace of Jesus—because Jesus is good and He loves us and wants us to live with Him.

Our perfect home is all ready. Won't it be fun to go to our new heavenly home?

If Adam and Eve were to come to your town this week, do you think you'd notice that they were "strangers on earth"? How would you know they were strangers?

Endnotes for Parents

"All Done!" is adapted from Genesis 1 and 2.

---

*You recognize in this paragraph a recounting of the events of the Creation week.

This is a story about ***grace.***

Grace is God preparing an eternal home for us long before we were born, even before He made our world (Eph. 1:4; 2 Tim. 1:9, 10). God could have said to us, "You're on your own. Here's some stuff to build with. Get to work. If you ever get over to My neighborhood, be sure to stop in for a visit."

In that case we could have tried to work our way to heaven or earn our heavenly home. But we would have failed.

Grace is the fact that the work is all done, everything is finished, everything is completed. Heaven is our home (Phil. 3:20). And our home is all ready for us.

Grace is the wonderful truth that Jesus already paid the price. He didn't pay part of it. He paid it all. We don't have to be afraid that we aren't good enough to have a home in heaven. Our heavenly home is ours because Jesus is good and because He loves us.

"'Surely God is my salvation; I will trust and not be afraid. The Lord, the Lord himself, is my strength and my defense; he has become my salvation.' With joy you will draw water from the wells of salvation" (Isa. 12:2, 3).

"Do not let your hearts be troubled. You believe in God; believe also in me. My Father's house has many rooms; if that were not so, would I have told you that I am going there to prepare a place for you? And if I go and prepare a place for you, I will come back and take you to be with me that you also may be where I am" (John 14:1-3).

"Compared to what's coming, living conditions around here seem like a stopover in an unfurnished shack, and we're tired of it! We've been given a glimpse of the real thing, our true home" (2 Cor. 5:2, Message).

A. Skib

2

The Lord Will Provide

"Is anything too hard for the Lord?"

Genesis 18:14.

Abraham celebrated his first birthday when he was 100 years old. How could he do that? Here's how. Just one year before, God had changed his name from Abram to Abraham. He had lived 99 years as Abram, but only one year as Abraham. That's how *Abraham* celebrated his first birthday at age 100. His new name meant "the father of many nations."

At the same time God changed the name of Abraham's wife, Sarai, to Sarah. Sarah was 10 years younger than Abraham, so she was 90. Her new name meant "the mother of nations."

But unfortunately Abraham and Sarah were not the father and mother of anyone. *Together* they had no children at all. And by now they were much too old to have children.[1] But the old couple did not give up hoping that one day they would have a baby, because God had taught them a very important lesson.

Nothing Is Too Hard for God

Abraham and Sarah had learned that God has the power to do what He promises. "Is anything too hard for the Lord?" Abraham would say to people who visited them.[2]

God had promised Abraham and Sarah that they would have a baby. It was the one promise that Abraham and Sarah most wanted to come true. And sure enough, just as God had said, Baby Isaac was born.

Isaac was the most precious thing in Abraham

and Sarah's life. Each time they told the story of Isaac's birth, everyone would laugh and laugh some more.[3] It was a very, very happy story. Abraham was as happy as he could be. He had the son God had promised him. He had a wonderful home. He had everything he wanted here on earth.

Wishing for a Better Home

But now old Abraham began to think about something else. He began wishing for a better country than the one where he lived. He wanted to get to his heavenly home. "I'm really just a stranger on this earth," he'd say. "I'd rather be in heaven."[4]

If Abraham was like the rest of us, he also began to wonder if God needed any help getting him to heaven. *I've tried to help God in the past,* Abraham may have thought. *I helped Him rescue Lot from the four kings. I tried to help God protect us from the pharaoh and from King Abimelech. I married Hagar to try to help God make me the father of many nations. I wonder what I need to do* now *to help God get me to heaven.*

A Strange Message From God

One morning, while Abraham was still wondering, something happened that people would talk about for the rest of history. God decided that there was only one way to teach Abraham a lesson about how to get to that better country called heaven. That morning God woke Abraham and gave him a very strange message.

"Take your son," God told him, "your only son, Isaac, whom you love. Travel to a mountain that I will show you. There on the mountaintop, build an altar of stones. On the top of the altar, place some wood. And then tie Isaac on top of the altar and give him to Me as a burnt offering."

Now, of course, God would never have allowed Abraham to do such a thing to his son. The Bible is very clear that God doesn't want any of us to be hurt. But Abraham didn't understand the lesson yet. All he wanted to do was get to that better country.

Maybe he thought, *So that's what I have to do to get to heaven. I have to give God the most precious thing in my life. I have to give up the very thing that makes me the happiest. If that's what God wants, I'll obey Him. Then God will know that I'm a really good person. Then God will reward me with heaven.*

We can't know for sure what was going on in Abraham's mind. But we do know that early the next morning Abraham woke Isaac to go on a long walk with him. They packed enough food to last several days. They packed wood for a fire. Then they saddled a donkey for Abraham to ride, and away they went.

God Provides the Sacrifice

Three days later Abraham stopped and squinted. In the distance he saw a mountain. It was the place God had shown him. So Abraham got off the donkey, and he and Isaac climbed to the top of the mountain. Abraham slowly built the altar, stone upon stone. He carefully arranged the wood so it would burst into fire. Then he turned to Isaac.

"Do you remember the question you asked me on the way up the mountain?" Abraham asked.

"I asked where the lamb was for the burnt offering," Isaac said.

"And do you remember my answer?"

"You said God would provide the lamb," Isaac said.

"Well, God has provided it. God told me that *you* should be the offering."

"What?" cried Isaac.

"God wants me to give you to Him as an offering," Abraham said.

"Father? Are you sure? Are you going to do it?"

"It's what God wants me to do. Then He'll know I'll obey Him. And then I'll be good enough to take to heaven," explained Abraham.

(Now, don't worry! This is going to turn out well. Remember that God did not really want Abraham to give Isaac as an offering. He just needed to teach Abraham a lesson.)

So Isaac climbed up on the altar, and Abraham tied him to the stones. Then Abraham picked up his knife and raised it above Isaac. His arm shook. In fact, he was shaking all over.

Suddenly a voice from heaven called his name.

"Stop, Abraham!" the voice shouted. "Don't lay a hand on the boy!"

At that the knife fell from Abraham's hand.

"I know your heart is right," God said to Abraham. "I know you obey Me. But there's a big, important lesson I need for you to learn."

"What lesson is that?" asked Abraham.

"Nothing you can do will help Me give you heaven," God told him. "You can't earn the right to live in heaven. You can't make Me love you any more than I already do, not even by being willing to give Me your son. What you said to Isaac was true, though. *I* provide the sacrifice that makes heaven yours. That's *My* job."

Suddenly the lesson was very clear. God has already given the gift of His grace. (Remember, *grace* means that God does good things for us because He is good and He loves us.) We don't have to help God keep His promises.

Now Abraham understood. Getting to heaven is about God's goodness, not ours. In honor of the lesson, Abraham gave the mountain a new name. He called it The Lord Will Provide.

What can we learn about being "a stranger on earth" from the story of Abraham?

Endnotes for Parents

"The Lord Will Provide"
is based on Genesis 22:1-18.

---

[1] Gen. 18:11.

[2] Verses 13, 14.

[3] Gen. 21:6.

[4] In the book of Hebrews, in between the story of Isaac's birth (Heb. 11:11, 12) and the story of Abraham binding Isaac (verses 17-19) is a paragraph that turns the story into a discussion of heavenly, eternal things (verses 13-16).

This is a story about ***grace.***

Grace assures us, whenever we're tempted to believe that God can't keep His promises, that nothing is too hard for the Lord.

Grace is the wonderful story of God giving His Son—His only Son, Jesus, whom He loved—so that we might know for sure that we already have eternal life.

Grace is God stopping every one of our efforts to win His favor and earn our way into heaven. ***Grace*** is God saying to us, "I provide the sacrifice."

"This is love: not that we loved God, but that he loved us and sent his Son as an atoning sacrifice for our sins" (1 John 4:10).

"Because of his great love for us, God, who is rich in mercy, made us alive with Christ even when we were dead in transgressions—it is by grace you have been saved" (Eph. 2:4, 5).

"He [the Lord] has sent me to bind up the brokenhearted, to proclaim freedom for the captives and release from darkness for the prisoners, . . . to bestow on them a crown of beauty instead of ashes, the oil of joy instead of mourning, and a garment of praise instead of a spirit of despair. They will be called oaks of righteousness, a planting of the Lord for the display of his splendor" (Isa. 61:1-3).

A. Skib

3

More Than Enough

"God has made me forget all my trouble."

Genesis 41:51.

Fat cows and skinny cows. This was not a happy dream for a man who thought he was a god. But there he was, the most powerful man in Egypt, sitting straight up in bed in the middle of the night. He was trying to figure out his dream about fat cows and skinny cows.

By morning the dream was driving Pharaoh crazy. "What does it mean?" he shouted to everyone in the palace. He couldn't eat. He couldn't concentrate. Every conversation turned to fat cows and skinny cows.

Then one of Pharaoh's servants came to the rescue. He remembered a man he'd met when he was in jail a few years before. "I had some terrible nightmares," he explained to Pharaoh. "This man, named Joseph, explained what they meant. My dreams came true just as Joseph said they would."

A Prisoner Comes to the Rescue

Pharaoh listened to this servant and then gave orders. Guards hurried to the jail and brought Joseph out. As fast as he could, he took a bath and shaved. He put on clean clothes. Then he was rushed to the palace to see the worried Pharaoh.

"Fat cows and skinny cows," Pharaoh moaned. He told Joseph every detail he could remember about his dream. "Tell me what it means," he commanded.

"I can't do that," Joseph said.

Suddenly the room got very quiet. No one in

Pharaoh's court had expected that answer.

"I can't explain your dream," Joseph said. "But the God of heaven can. He will tell us what it means."

Then suddenly the meaning of the dream was clear to Joseph. Egypt would have seven great years when the land would grow plenty of food—more food than the people could possibly eat. That was the fat-cow part. Everyone would be rich. Everyone's fields would produce big crops. The good years would make people in other countries wish they lived in Egypt.

But the good times would be followed by seven very bad years. That was what the part about the skinny cows meant. All the crops would die. People would go hungry. Animals would starve. It would be so bad that no one would remember the good times. The bad times would almost ruin Egypt. Other people would be very thankful they *didn't* live in Egypt.

"God in heaven gave me the meaning of the dream," Joseph told the king. Then he told Pharaoh what he should do.

"During the time of plenty, take part of the grain and save it for later," Joseph said. "Put the extra grain in big storehouses in the cities. Don't let anyone use the grain until the bad times come. Then share the stored grain, little by little, to save the people."

Joseph Gets a New Job

Pharaoh immediately saw the good sense in what Joseph said. "Your plan is brilliant!" Pharaoh said. "Now I need someone to put this plan into action. Joseph, I want you to do it!" Just that quickly Joseph had an important new job. The former prisoner was now second in command of "the whole land of Egypt."[1]

A ring showing his authority was placed on Joseph's finger. A robe of fine linen replaced his old prison robes. A gold chain was placed around his neck. Joseph was given a chariot to ride in. Important people walked ahead of him, telling everyone that Joseph was now in charge.

The Dream Comes True

The dream about fat cows and skinny cows came true exactly as God had told Joseph it would.

First came the good years. No other Egyptian good time had ever brought such riches. For seven years the grain fields produced huge harvests. The farmers couldn't keep up with all the grain. Their donkeys groaned under the weight of the wheat. The storerooms bulged to the breaking point. Every day the smell of freshly baked bread filled every corner of every home in every part of the countryside.

The land produced *way more than enough.* The Bible says that grain piled up "like the sand of the sea; it was so much that he [Joseph] stopped keeping records because it was beyond measure."[2]

And then the seven years of plenty came to an end. The "skinny cows" showed up. The bad years came.

The rain didn't fall. The river Nile didn't flood its banks. The farmers couldn't plant their crops. The fields couldn't produce wheat. There were no harvests. The donkeys had nothing to carry. The trips to take extra grain to the storehouses stopped. There was no grain to grind into flour to bake bread. The people started getting hungry. Before long most of them couldn't even remember the good years.[3]

The people of Egypt came to Joseph. They asked him to help them during the hard times. That was exactly what Joseph wanted to do. He opened the storehouses and gave them grain. The people went home and made bread once again.

But the hard times got worse. The bad weather spread to other countries. When "the famine was severe *everywhere*," people from many countries came to Egypt[4] to get grain from Joseph. The plan God gave to Joseph worked amazingly well. Egypt had more than enough grain to share. No matter how awful the bad times got, there was always enough grain to feed everyone. God had given them everything they needed and more!

Another Surprise for Joseph

Then something happened that even Joseph never could have dreamed of. The famine was bad all the way up in the land of Canaan. That's the place where Joseph had been born and where he had lived until he was 17 years old.[5] Joseph's aging father, Jacob, and all of his brothers were hungry too. "I hear that there is grain for sale in Egypt," Jacob said during the second year of the famine.[6] "Go down to Egypt and buy grain for us there, that we may survive and not die."[7]

So the "skinny cows," the seven years of hunger, ended up leading to a big family reunion. Joseph and his brothers and their father, after many years of being apart, were together again. After much hugging and kissing, Joseph said to his family, "God sent me here so I could preserve your lives here in Egypt."[8]

God takes even the "skinny cows," even the bad times, and turns them into good.

Joseph gave God the credit for explaining Pharaoh's dream. How does this help us know that Joseph was "a stranger on earth"?

Endnotes for Parents

"More Than Enough"
is based on Genesis 41-45.

---

[1] Gen. 41:41-43.
[2] Verse 49.
[3] Verse 31.
[4] Verse 57.
[5] Gen. 37:2.
[6] Gen. 45:6.
[7] Gen. 42:2.
[8] Gen. 45:5, 7.

This is a story of ***grace.***

We never need to ask if there is enough ***grace*** to forgive our frequent failures, to pursue us in our wayward wanderings, to sustain us in our severe famines, or to take us all the way home to heaven. ***Grace*** is unquantifiable. It is beyond measure. ***Grace*** is ours in *abundance!*

We "drink deeply" of God's "overflowing *abundance*" of ***grace***. We are continuously filled, constantly delighted, and completely satisfied (Isa. 66:7-11).

Grace, like biblical *abundance*, is more than just surplus. It is *beyond measure*. It keeps filling us. It meets all of our needs. It is so big it provides plenty for all of the countries in the entire world.

"Praise our God, all peoples, let the sound of his praise be heard; he has preserved our lives and kept our feet from slipping. . . . We went through fire and water, but [he] brought us to a place of abundance" (Ps. 66:8-12).

"Grace and peace be yours in abundance through the knowledge of God and of Jesus our Lord" (2 Peter 1:2).

A. Skib

4

The Bush That Wouldn't Burn Up

"I will be with you."

Exodus 3:12.

"I am a stranger in a foreign land," Moses complained one day in a lonely mood.[1] "I miss my mother and my father. I miss my sister and my brother. I miss my old friends. I miss the food I used to enjoy eating. I even miss the hippos and the crocodiles in the river Nile. There's nothing around here but these silly sheep! And they don't even belong to me." (The sheep belonged to his father-in-law, Jethro.)[2]

Moses was not very happy.

Once upon a time, when he was a boy growing up to be a young man, Moses had lived in the capital city of Egypt. He had lived in a beautiful palace with the princess, who had adopted him. At the palace Moses had plenty of good food to eat and a comfortable bed to sleep on. There was sweet music playing in the background and beautiful art painted on the walls. There were even servants who swooshed away the flies and got Moses anything he wanted.

But that was many years ago. Now he lived in a tent in the middle of a desert. *It's too hot in this desert,* Moses must have thought. *There's never enough water to drink. The food is always the same. The desert snakes are angry. The desert flies are pesky. The desert people are unfriendly.*[3] *I really am a stranger in a foreign land.*

Even the Bushes Burn

One day Moses wandered with the sheep to the far side of the desert. They stopped near a mountain named Horeb. The water was warm. His lunch was bitter. All around him were the silly sheep, the angry snakes, and the pesky flies. The weather was hot and dry.

Then all of a sudden, on the side of the mountain, Moses saw a bush that had burst into flames.

It's just too *hot*, Moses must have thought. *Now even the desert bushes are burning up.*

But as Moses stared at the bush, he noticed something very unusual. The bush did *not* burn up! It was definitely on fire. Its leaves were burning. Its branches were blazing. There was a big, bright flame right in the middle of the bush. But the bush didn't burn up.

"I'm going to get closer," Moses said to himself. "I'm going to figure out what's going on here. How can this strange bush not burn up?"

Moses began to walk straight toward the bush. The silly sheep quit munching on the grasses and followed him. The pesky flies buzzed around his sweaty head. Moses got closer and closer. He heard the leaves crackling in the fire. He smelled the branches sizzling in the flames. He could feel his hands and face getting hotter and hotter.

Moses Gets a Big Surprise

Suddenly a great big voice broke the desert silence. The voice was calling his name.

"Moses! Moses!"

Moses looked to the right. No one was there. He looked to the left. There was nobody for miles and miles. He spun around quickly and looked behind him. He was all alone. Who was talking? How did the voice know his name?

"Here I am," Moses said, still wondering whom he was talking to.

"Stop where you are," the voice commanded. "Don't come any closer. Bend over and take off your sandals. You are standing on holy ground."

Moses didn't quite understand. But he did exactly what the voice told him to do. He was too afraid to do anything else. And the moment his bare feet came in contact with the hot desert sand, Moses got another big surprise. The sand in front of the bush wasn't hot at all. It didn't burn his feet. It must have felt cool and refreshing, almost as if he were standing on the papyrus reeds that grew along the banks of the river Nile back in Egypt.

Then the voice told Moses who He was.

"I am the God of your fathers," the voice explained. "I am the God of Abraham. The God of Isaac. And the God of Jacob."

So that's why the bush was burning. That's why the flame was blazing. That's why the ground was holy. God was there.

A New Job for Moses

Suddenly Moses got very serious. He bowed down and hid his face behind his hands.

Was God angry with him because he had complained about living in the desert? Was God upset? After all, God had needed to come all the way out to the far side of the desert to talk to him.

No, that wasn't it at all! God was looking for a man to lead His people, the Israelites, out of their cruel slavery in Egypt. Moses was just the person God wanted.

"I am sending you to Pharaoh to tell him to let My people go," God told Moses from the middle of the flaming bush.

"Who? Me?" Moses asked in surprise. All of a sudden he felt small and shy. "You want *me* to go *where*? I've been gone too long. I can't go back."

"Yes, you can," God said calmly.

"But the Egyptians have their own gods. They don't know You. And the Israelites have forgotten You. What's more, they think You have forgotten them."

"The leaders of Israel will listen to you," God told him. "Tell them I haven't forgotten them at all. I've been watching. I've been listening. I know they have been suffering. Now I will rescue them."

"What if they don't believe me?" Moses argued. "What if they think I've spent too much time out in the hot desert sun?"

Suddenly God asked Moses a question. "What is that in your hand?"

"It's my staff," Moses answered. "I use it to guide the silly sheep."

"Throw it on the ground," God said.

So Moses threw his staff down on the ground. In an instant the staff turned into one of those angry desert snakes. Moses started to run away.

"Wait!" God called. "Now reach down and pick the snake up by the tail."

"If I pick it up by the tail," Moses gasped, "it will turn around and bite me."

"Do what I say," God said. His voice reminded Moses who was in charge.

So Moses walked carefully to the snake. He got behind it, then reached down quickly and grabbed its tail. Just like that, the snake became his staff again. *It's a miracle!* Moses thought.

"OK," Moses said. He was starting to realize he shouldn't argue with God. "But I should tell You I'm not very good at speaking. I get nervous. My tongue kind of gets stuck to the roof of my mouth."

"Who made your tongue?" God asked. "And who made people's ears? And where do you think people got their eyes? I made all those things. You go to Egypt. I'll be with you. I'll help you speak and teach you what to say. And don't forget to take your staff. Sometimes My people act like silly sheep. Your staff will come in handy when you lead them out of Egypt."[4]

So Moses gave a big sigh and agreed to his new job. Slowly he walked back across the hot desert to the home where he lived with his wife and their two boys. He told them about the burning bush and about God talking to him. So they all packed their bags and headed toward Egypt.

The really big story in Moses' life was just beginning.

What did Moses learn at the bush that wouldn't burn up about being "a stranger on earth"?

Endnotes for Parents

"The Bush That Wouldn't Burn Up" is based on Exodus 2:15-4:20.

---

[1] Ex. 2:22.
[2] Ex. 3:1.
[3] Ex. 2:16-19.
[4] Ex. 4:17.

This is a story about ***grace.***

Whenever we're afraid, ***grace*** reminds us that God knows what we're going through. He hasn't forgotten us. He's been watching. He's been listening. He knows.

Grace teaches us that our story is not about how strong we are or how much courage we have. The real story is about how big and courageous God is.

"Can a mother forget the baby at her breast and have no compassion on the child she has borne? Though she may forget, I will not forget you! See, I have engraved you on the palms of my hands" (Isa. 49:15, 16).

A. Skib

5

New Words in the Desert

"How happy you must be—
you get a fresh start."

Psalm 32:1, Message.

The children of Israel lived in Egypt for a very long time. During all those years they quit singing happy songs. They quit writing stories with happy endings. They quit dancing their happy dances. Instead, they learned some unhappy new words.

One of the words they learned was "slavery." Before they were forced to be slaves in Egypt, Israelite families sang and danced and sat around their campfires. They told happy stories to one another. Some of the stories were about times that God had helped them in the past.

They were free people. They could come and go whenever they liked. They worked for themselves. They tended their gardens and took care of their flocks of sheep.

But now the Israelites worked for the Egyptians and did only what the Egyptians wanted them to do. The Egyptians needed bricks to build their huge buildings. So the Israelites made bricks.

The Israelites also learned the words "hard labor." Before they became slaves, the Israelites would get up in the morning, have breakfast, and sit around the table talking to one another. But the Egyptians wanted their bricks right now! So the Israelites had to get up very early and run to the brickmaking place. There they would work all day long in the hot sun with hardly a break to eat. They'd work until long after the sun went down to make enough bricks. Then they'd drag themselves home and fall into bed, exhausted.

Another word the Israelites learned in Egypt

was "taskmaster." The Egyptians put bosses in charge of the Israelites to make sure they got up early, got to work quickly, and got all the bricks made. If an Israelite got up late, the taskmaster would call him lazy and push him out the door. If an Israelite didn't work hard enough, the taskmaster would hit him with a whip. The taskmasters were mean. They made the lives of the Israelites miserable. The Israelites wished they had never heard the word "taskmaster."[1]

Soon the Israelites learned another word: "groaning."[2] They were tired and hungry. They worked so hard that they hurt all over. They had no hope of a happier life. They complained and grumbled and cried out loud.

New Words for a New Start

But then Moses arrived! He was fresh from his talk with God at the bush that wouldn't burn up. Moses brought hope to God's people. He told the king of Egypt that the Israelites were not going to be slaves any longer. They were not going to make any more bricks. No more hard labor. No more taskmasters. No more groaning.

Moses led the Israelites out of Egypt into the desert. They walked through the Red Sea on dry ground. They sang happy songs about God rescuing them, and they danced to the music. They told happy stories to one another. They camped under palm trees and drank fresh water.[3] And they started to learn some new words.

One of their first new words was "manna." No one had ever used that word before to talk about food. But now they used the word to talk about what they ate every day. In the morning they would wake up to find delicious breadlike food waiting for them all around their tents. It was as if God had rained down bread from heaven.[4] Each family gathered just enough manna to last one day.

But on Fridays there was extra manna on the ground. That was for them to eat on Sabbath, when manna did not come. The people didn't have to gather their food on that special day. The manna left over from Friday stayed fresh and good for them to eat on Sabbath. "Manna" was a tasty new word they learned.

God at the Center of the Camp

Another new word was "sanctuary." God wanted the people to see that He was living with them in their camp. He told Moses to build a beautiful big tent and call it the sanctuary. Then Moses organized the whole camp with the sanctuary in the center.

The sanctuary had three main parts. The first part was a big courtyard. Everyone in the camp was welcome to come to the courtyard. In the courtyard were three important places. One was the place the people brought their offerings. At the second place the priests, who worked like the pastors in your church, cleaned the offerings. And at the third place the offerings were given to God.

The second part of the sanctuary was the first room inside the tent itself. The room was called the *holy place*. Only the priests entered this room. On the south side of the room the priests kept seven oil lamps burning all day and all night. Across the room was a table with 12 fresh loaves of flatbread. All the people in the camp belonged to one of 12 big families, or tribes. That meant each tribe always had a loaf of fresh bread in the holy place. And there was a little altar where sweet-smelling incense always burned.

The third part of the sanctuary was called the *Most Holy Place*. Only the high priest could go into that room, and then only one time every year. There was a golden chest in the room called the *ark of the promise*. Two carved angels stood on top of the chest. At that very sacred place God would talk to the high priest about the Israelites.

In one of those talks in the Most Holy Place God taught the high priest the very happy word "atonement." Let's see if we can understand this big word.

Lesson From a Smashed Bicycle

Imagine you are outside riding your bicycle when your mom calls you to come into the house for supper. You leave your bicycle next to the curb in front of your house. A few minutes later something awful happens. A teenage boy from a few houses away gets into a car with his father. The boy is just learning how to drive, and he starts to drive down the street. When he gets in front of your house, the boy accidentally turns the car to the curb and drives right over your bike! He slams on the brakes, but it's too late. The boy and his dad jump out of the car to see the damage.

At the same time you and your mom hear the brakes squealing. You stop eating and rush out to see what's happened. The boy's mother hears the same thing and runs down the street to see if everything is OK.

All of you bend over and pick up the pieces of your bicycle. It's totally ruined. The tires are smashed. The frame is twisted. The seat is wrecked. The handlebars are broken. Your bike cannot be fixed. A little tear comes to your eye. The boy is sorry, but he doesn't have the money to buy a new bike for you. Now what?

The boy's mother comes to the rescue. "Don't worry," she says to her son. "We all make mistakes while we're learning to drive. We'll take care of it."

The mom and dad get back in the car with their son. This time Dad does the driving. They drive into town and in just a few minutes come back with a brand-new bike they've bought for you. In fact, this bike is even better than the one that was smashed. You're happy! The boy is happy! Everyone is happy. Everything turned out well.

The boy made a mistake. He was sorry for what he had done. The mother and father forgave their boy for the mistake. And then they *made atonement* for the mistake. They fixed the problem he had caused. They paid for the new bike because their son couldn't pay for it himself.

The new word "atonement" made the Israelites very happy indeed. They began to understand that Jesus forgives us when we make mistakes. What's more, He makes atonement. He fixes our problem because we can't fix it ourselves. Jesus makes things even better than they were in the first place.

What is there about forgiveness that makes us want to be "strangers on earth"?

Endnotes for Parents

"New Words in the Desert" is built on passages in Exodus 1:8-22; 5:4-21; 15; 16; and 25-27.

---

[1] Ex. 1:11-14; 2:11, 23.
[2] Ex. 2:23, 24; 6:5.
[3] Ex. 15:1-27.
[4] Ex. 16:4; Ps. 78:24.

This is a story about ***grace.***

Grace realizes that we all make mistakes "while we're learning to drive." ***Grace*** forgives us for our mistakes and makes atonement.

Grace does for us that which is impossible for us to do for ourselves. It pays the price. It makes us right with God again.

"The priest will make atonement for them before the Lord, and they will be forgiven for any of the things they did that made them guilty" (Lev. 6:7).

"God presented Christ as a sacrifice of atonement, through the shedding of his blood—to be received by faith. He did this to demonstrate his righteousness" (Rom. 3:25).

"In him we have redemption through his blood, the forgiveness of sins, in accordance with the riches of God's grace" (Eph. 1:7).

A. Skib

6

Too Many Soldiers

"Stand still and see this great thing the Lord is about to do."

1 Samuel 12:16.

The Israelites had escaped from Egypt. God had led them through the desert to their new home in the land of Canaan. But now the Israelites were acting badly again.

They forgot all the good things God had done for them. Only a few remembered how God had rescued them from slavery in Egypt. Fewer still remembered the miracles God had done in the desert. They stopped thinking about the manna that had fed them, the water that had flowed from the rock, and the pillar of fire that had warmed them at night.

When God told them what direction to go, the people went the opposite way. They tried to be like the people of Canaan, who didn't believe in God. They did business with the Canaanites. They ate the same food the Canaanite people ate. They married Canaanites. They sneaked off into the woods and bowed down to Canaanite idols made of wood and stone.[1] They were stubborn and dishonest. They quarreled with each other.[2] Every person made up their own rules.[3]

What's more, the Israelites were scared. Their enemies attacked them from every direction—north, south, east, and west. The enemies brought horses and chariots and all their troops.[4] It seemed that there were as many enemy soldiers as grains of sand on the seashore.

When the Israelites planted their crops, their enemies raced in and ripped up all the gardens and tore up all the fields. They stole the Israelites' sheep and cows and donkeys. The enemy soldiers took

away the Israelites' swords and spears.[5] All the Israelites had left to defend themselves were hammers and axes. The enemies swarmed over the land like grasshoppers. They had so many camels that the Israelites couldn't even count them all.

But when the Israelites weren't fighting, they were tiptoeing around the corner to worship idols. When they weren't sneaking away to the idols, they were hiding from their enemies. They hid in secret places in the mountains. They stayed out of sight in the valleys. They found hiding places in caves. And they took cover behind the walls of their little forts.[6] But their enemies always found them.

The Angel of the Lord Appears

One day an Israelite named Gideon was hiding from some enemies called the Midianites. Gideon had stacked rocks in a circle to hold the juice that came out when he stomped on great big piles of grapes. But Gideon wasn't stomping grapes now. He was bending down behind the low wall, threshing a small amount of wheat. He used a pitchfork to throw the wheat up in the air. Again and again he'd lift forkfuls of wheat and let it fall to the ground. The breezes blew away the parts that he couldn't eat, leaving the grains of wheat that he wanted to keep.

Usually the Israelites threshed wheat out in the open. But Gideon was afraid to be out in the open. He was hiding behind the little wall, hoping the Midianites wouldn't find him.

All of a sudden Gideon was not alone. The angel of the Lord came from heaven and sat under a tree next to Gideon's hiding place. But Gideon didn't notice the angel.

Then the angel spoke. "The Lord is with you, mighty warrior!" he said.

Gideon was startled. Who was this stranger, and why was he saying that the Lord was with him? Why was he calling Gideon a mighty warrior when he was actually hiding up in the mountains? *Is he making fun of me?* Gideon wondered.

"Excuse me," Gideon said. He felt a little annoyed. "If the Lord is with us, why do our enemies keep defeating us? Why isn't God still doing the wonderful things that our grandfathers said He used to do? It seems to me that God has walked away from us and left us on our own."

But the angel ignored Gideon's questions. Instead, he gave this command: "Go in the strength you have and save the Israelites from the Midianites."

"Excuse me again," Gideon shot back. "How could I possibly save the Israelites? My family is the weakest family in all of this territory. And even in my family nobody thinks I'm very important. Don't forget, I'm up here hiding!"

"You will go because I will send you," the angel said. "You will succeed because I will be with you. You *will* defeat the Midianites. Don't be afraid."

Gideon Begins at Home

That very night Gideon began to do what the angel told him to do. Quietly Gideon and 10 of his friends went into the woods and tore down the altar that had been built to worship a Canaanite god called Baal. In its place he built an altar to worship God on top of the hill. Then he cut down an idol made of wood and used the wood to build a fire to offer a sacrifice to God.

The next morning people in the village were angry. "Who tore down the altar to our god Baal?" they shouted. "Whoever did this is going to have to pay!"

Gideon's father, Joash, answered the people of the village.

"Are you really going to argue for Baal?" Joash asked. "Are you actually trying to save this idol? If Baal is a true god, he doesn't need you. He can defend himself when someone smashes his altar."

The people backed away. They knew Joash was telling the truth.

Gideon remembered what the angel had promised. He began to ask people to join him in fighting the Midianites. In village after village

Israelite men said yes to Gideon's call. Before long Gideon had 50 people ready to fight. Then 75 soldiers were ready. Soon hundreds had joined the army. Then thousands caught the spirit. In a matter of days 32,000 Israelites had come out from their hiding places to join Gideon.

Too Many Soldiers

But God was not happy with thousands of troops.

"You have too many soldiers," God said to Gideon. "If all those soldiers help you defeat the Midianites, you'll say you did it all by yourself. Cut down the number of soldiers. Send home anyone who is afraid of the upcoming battle."

Twenty-two thousand men admitted they were afraid, so Gideon told them they could go back to their homes. Now the army numbered 10,000. It was still a very big army.

"You still have too many soldiers," God said. "Gideon, send more men home."

So another 9,700 soldiers were sent away. Now they were down to only 300.

"We don't have enough men to defeat the Midianites," one soldier must have said. "The enemy has so many soldiers we can't even count them."

"We don't even have weapons," another Israelite complained. "How can we win?"

But Gideon divided his men again. This time he formed them into three little groups of just 100 soldiers each. Then Gideon gave them their weapons for the battle. Can you guess what they were?

Gideon didn't give them swords, and he didn't give them bows and arrows. Instead each soldier carried a trumpet in one hand. In the other hand each soldier held a clay jar with a burning torch inside. The jar covered the flame so no one could see it.

"When we get to the edge of the Midianite camp," Gideon whispered, "watch me and do exactly what I do."

The Israelites attacked just after midnight. They smashed the jars and held up their torches. Then they blew their trumpets and shouted as loudly as they could.

The Midianites woke up suddenly and panicked. Every enemy soldier ran away as fast as they could. None of the Israelites even had to fight. And the Midianite army never came back again.[7] The Lord had defeated the enemy, just as He had promised.

How does Gideon's army remind us of the way God saves the "strangers on earth"?

Endnotes for Parents

You can find the original "Too Many Soldiers" story in Judges 6 and 7.

---

[1] Judges 3:26; Deut. 29:17.
[2] Judges 8 and 12.
[3] Judges 21:25.
[4] Judges 3:8, 12; 10; 3:31; 4:3; Joshua 11:4.
[5] 1 Sam. 13:19-21.
[6] Judges 6:2.
[7] Judges 8:28.

This is a story about ***grace.***

Grace is not about what God can do with 300 dedicated people. ***Grace*** is what God does when the situation is *impossible.* Three hundred against an innumerable army is an impossible state of affairs. When our chances of success are impossible, that's when ***grace*** takes over.

Grace reminds us we are mighty only in God's strength.

"'Not by might nor by power, but by my Spirit,' says the Lord Almighty" (Zech. 4:6).

"Woe to those who go down to Egypt for help, who rely on horses, who trust in the multitude of their chariots and in the great strength of their horsemen, but do not look to the Holy One of Israel, or seek help from the Lord" (Isa. 31:1).

A. Skib

7

Hannah's Happy Song

"The Lord has filled my heart with joy; how happy I am."

1 Samuel 2:1, TEV.

Do you live anywhere near a desert? Have you ever walked on ground that's covered with rocks and hot sand? Have you seen land so dry that only scrub bushes and cactus plants can grow in it? It seems that only snakes and scorpions, lizards and buzzards like to live in the hot, dry desert.

When we talk about deserts we use words such as dry, hot, bare, empty, and barren. "Barren" means nothing grows there. Not very many people want to live in a place like that, do they? Most of us like to have water and trees, grass and flowers, cool breezes, and lots of friends living nearby.

But the people of the Old Testament spent a lot of time living in the desert. Abraham had to cross a huge, dry desert to get to the land of Canaan. In Egypt only the land along the river Nile was not dusty desert. The freed Israelite slaves wandered in the desert for 40 years before they got to the Promised Land. The children of Israel knew deserts well.

Jeremiah reminded them that God had led them "through the barren wilderness, through a land of deserts and ravines, a land of drought and utter darkness, a land where no one travels and no one lives" (Jer. 2:6).

When God wanted to remind the Israelites about His goodness, He often talked to them about deserts. "I will make rivers flow on barren heights," God promised. "I will turn the desert into pools of water, and the parched ground into

springs. I will put [trees] in the desert . . . so that people may see and know . . . that the hand of the Lord has done this, that the Holy One of Israel has created it" (Isa. 41:18-20).

Barren People, Too

Sometimes the Bible compared people to deserts. When they were hot and tired, when they were thirsty, or when they acted foolish, God compared them to dry, empty deserts.[1]

People especially used the word "barren" when a husband and wife didn't have any babies.[2] Ever since God had told Adam and Eve to be "fruitful and increase in number,"[3] most people thought it was a big blessing to have lots of children.[4] So not having any children made husbands and wives very sad.

Elkanah and Hannah were a husband and wife who lived not too long after Gideon's battle with the Midianites. They were very sad, for they wanted to have children together. But years passed, and no babies came. Whenever Hannah thought about it, she would cry. Sometimes she got so sad that she wouldn't eat. Once a year Elkanah and Hannah went to Shiloh to worship at the sanctuary. And every year Hannah asked God to give her the blessing of children.

One day Hannah had a long talk with Eli, the high priest in the sanctuary. Eli felt sad for Hannah and tried to help her smile. When they said goodbye, Eli prayed for Hannah. "Now go in peace," Eli said. "May the God of Israel give you what you have been asking for."

The words cheered Hannah. She thanked Eli. She left the sanctuary and found something to eat. And she started smiling much more.[5]

The Blessing Arrives

And wouldn't you know it? That year a baby arrived at Hannah and Elkanah's home! After all those years of waiting, the blessing finally had come. Suddenly Hannah's food tasted really, really good. She seemed to be hungry all the time. And after all those tears, happy smiles now shone on Hannah's face.

They named the little boy Samuel. He had big eyes and long, dark hair that his parents would never cut. Hannah was so happy she started singing. But she wasn't thinking about deserts anymore. Hannah didn't sing about snakes or scorpions or hot desert sand. She didn't use the words "empty" or "dry" in her song. Hannah only used words that were happy. She sang her song everywhere she went.

"The weapons of the strong are smashed to pieces," Hannah sang, "while the weak are infused with fresh strength. The well-fed are out begging in the streets for crusts, while the hungry are getting second helpings. The barren woman has a houseful of children" (1 Sam. 2:4, 5, Message).

A Baby With a Special Mission

Hannah stayed home with Samuel the next time her husband went on his yearly visit to the sanctuary at Shiloh. But the next year Hannah and Samuel both went along.

"Remember me?" Hannah said to Eli. "I'm

the woman who was crying here a couple of years ago and praying for the blessing of children. You spoke to me and made me happy. Well, look what I have now!" Hannah held little Samuel up so Eli could see her precious boy. Hannah might even have sung her song for the old high priest.

"You're not crying now, are you?" said Eli. "No more tears!"

"No tears, only smiles," answered Hannah. "I'm so thankful. Now I want to dedicate Samuel so that he will serve God all his life."

And so Hannah and Elkanah, little Samuel, and Eli had a very special dedication ceremony. Eli held Samuel close and asked God to bless him right then and all through his life.

Samuel grew up to be a mighty leader of the people of Israel. God began talking to him while he was still a little boy. When Samuel spoke to the people, everyone listened. They knew he had been talking with God. Everyone in Israel recognized Samuel as a prophet.[6] He also became their judge, leading the whole country in times of trouble.[7] It was Samuel who set aside Saul to be Israel's first king. And it was Samuel who first heard God's voice in choosing David to be king.

Meanwhile, Hannah kept on being joyful. Her smile grew bigger and bigger from year to year. She gave birth to three more boys and two girls. Imagine Hannah's happy songs with all those blessings in her house!

How does Hannah's happy song remind us that she was "a stranger on earth"?

Endnotes for Parents

"Hannah's Happy Song" is taken from 1 Samuel 1 and 2.

---

[1] See, for example, Ps. 143:6 and Jer. 17:6.

[2] Gen. 11:30; 25:21; 29:31; Judges 13:2, 3; and Luke 1:5-7.

[3] Gen. 1:28.

[4] Notice how these two thoughts come together in Jewish understanding: "He will love you and bless you and increase your numbers. He will bless the fruit of your womb, the crops of your land—your grain, new wine and olive oil—the calves of your herds and the lambs of your flocks in the land he swore to your ancestors to give you. You will be blessed more than any other people; none of your men or women will be childless" (Deut. 7:13, 14).

[5] 1 Sam. 1:17, 18.

[6] 1 Sam. 3:19-21.

[7] 1 Sam. 7:6.

This is a story about ***grace.***

Grace describes how God blesses us with something we don't already have. We don't possess eternal life. God gives it to us as a loving gift.

Grace inspires us to enjoy all the good things in life here on earth—our families, our food, our many blessings—and to start singing about how good God is to us.

"He raises the poor from the dust and lifts the needy from the ash heap; he seats them with princes, with the princes of his people. He settles the childless woman in her home as a happy mother of children" (Ps. 113:7-9).

"I will give thanks to the Lord because of his righteousness; I will sing praise to the name of the Lord Most High" (Ps. 7:17).

"I will sing of the Lord's great love forever; with my mouth I will make your faithfulness known through all generations. I will declare that your love stands firm forever, that you have established your faithfulness in heaven itself" (Ps. 89:1, 2).

A.Skib

8

Jonathan's Secret Plan

"Nothing can keep him [God] from giving us the victory."
1 Samuel 14:6, TEV.

The soldiers in King Saul's army were so afraid they were shaking. The Philistine army was on the move again. And this time they were bringing 3,000 chariots to help them fight against Israel.

As soon as the soldiers of Israel saw the Philistine army, they began to run. Some ran to the north. Some ran to the south. Some ran to the east, all the way across the Jordan River. But the Philistines soldiers were everywhere. There seemed to be as many of them as grains of sand at the beach.

"Maybe if I hide in a cave," one soldier said, "the Philistines won't be able to find me."

"I'm going to jump into a well," said another. "They'll never find me there."

"I'm going to dive into the thornbushes," another soldier told his buddy. "Even if they see me, they won't come in after me."

"If we just had new swords," complained one young soldier, "then we could fight."

But there were no swords for Israel's army. There were no spears. The Philistines had made sure that the army of Israel didn't have weapons. They had taken away all the blacksmiths who could make weapons. All the Israelites had to fight with were the tools from their farms. And no one wanted to fight the Philistines with pitchforks and hammers. All they could do was tremble and hide—and hope that jumping into thornbushes would keep them safe.

Something Had to Be Done

But one day a young man named Jonathan decided that something had to be done. Jonathan was the son of King Saul. Early in the morning, before the other soldiers were awake, Jonathan woke up and got dressed. He didn't stop to tell his father where he was going. He didn't wake up his friends and try to talk them into going with him. The only other person who knew what Jonathan was doing was the young man who carried his armor. The two of them quietly slipped out of camp.

"I have a plan," Jonathan told his armor-bearer. "The Philistine army is camped on the other side of the mountain. We can get to the camp quickly if we take the pass between the mountains. Now, I'm sure there are guards watching from the cliffs on the north and south of the pass. But I believe that God will give us victory over them. With the Lord fighting for us, it doesn't matter that there are just two of us. Nothing can stop Him from saving us."

The armor-bearer agreed. "Let's do it!" he said. "I'm with you heart and soul."

"Here's my plan," whispered Jonathan. "When we get to the cliffs, it will already be light. If the guards on the cliffs are awake, they'll see us right away. If they say to us, 'Stand still right where you are; we'll come down to see you,' then that's what we'll do. We'll stay where we are and not climb the mountain.

"But if they say to us, 'Climb up the mountain and talk to us,' that will be the sign that God has given us victory over them."

Jonathan Attacks

By the time they had agreed on the secret plan, Jonathan and his armor-bearer had reached the pass. The sun shone brightly in the sky. The two brave Israelites walked out into the open and were immediately seen by the Philistine guards.

The guards began to laugh. "Look," they

yelled to each other, "the Hebrews are crawling out of their hiding places." The guards shouted down to Jonathan, "Why don't you climb up the mountain and talk to us? We'll teach you a lesson."

Jonathan and his armor-bearer looked at each other. Those were the words they had agreed on in their secret plan. "Climb up after me," Jonathan said softly. "The Lord has given us victory over them."

The Philistines didn't wait for the two Israelites to reach the top of the mountain. The guards thought they could use a surprise attack and defeat the two soldiers while they were still climbing. Twenty Philistine guards attacked in a small space. But Jonathan and his friend were confident in God's victory, and the Philistines were quickly defeated.

Other Philistine guards were watching from the top of the cliffs. When they saw that Jonathan and his armor-bearer had won the battle, they panicked. They shouted down to alert the soldiers in the Philistine camp. The soldiers in the camp began to panic as well. The Philistine officers panicked. Even the chariot drivers panicked. They began to shout at each other and hit at each other. They pulled out their swords and began to fight with each other.

And then they started to run. They ran to the north and they ran to the south. They ran to the east and they ran to the west. There were so many Philistines running that the ground shook as if an earthquake were taking place. The Philistine soldiers hid in the caves. They jumped in the wells. They even dove into the thornbushes!

The King Learns About Grace

Just at that moment King Saul and his small, frightened army arrived at the site of the battle. They looked with amazement on the scene. There was Jonathan standing next to his armor-bearer, watching the enemy run away. The Philistines were hitting each other with their swords as they tried to get away from Jonathan.

The soldiers of Israel knew it had been a day of grace. "This day the Lord has rescued us," they said.

Jonathan and his armor-bearer agreed. "It is the Lord who gives His people the victory. Nothing can stop Him from saving us."

How did Jonathan and his armor-bearer show that they were "strangers on earth"?

Endnotes for Parents

You can find "Jonathan's Secret Plan" in 1 Samuel 13 and 14.

This is a story about ***grace.***

Grace comes to us when we're shaking with fear, when we're afraid that eternal life is out of the question, when the only strength we have is the strength to try to hide from God. (Isn't that a silly picture!) ***Grace*** is God's assurance that nothing will stop Him from saving us.

Grace is the gift God gives us. It helps to accept the gift when we don't have our hands full of weapons.

Grace is what motivates God to rescue us when we can't rescue ourselves.

When we don't have ***grace***, all that's left to us is panic, confusion, and fear. ***Grace*** is what keeps us from running away from God.

"God is love. Whoever lives in love lives in God, and God in them. This is how love is made complete among us so that we will have confidence on the day of judgment: In this world we are like Jesus. There is no fear in love. But perfect love drives out fear" (1 John 4:16-18).

"I will praise you more and more. My mouth will tell of your righteous deeds, of your saving acts all day long—though I know not how to relate them all. I will come and proclaim your mighty acts, Sovereign Lord; I will proclaim your righteous deeds, yours alone" (Ps. 71:14-16).

"In that day they will say, 'Surely this is our God; we trusted in him, and he saved us. This is the Lord, we trusted in him; let us rejoice and be glad in his salvation'" (Isa. 25:9).

A. Skib

9

The Meanest Man in the Army

"It is not by sword or spear that the Lord saves."

1 Samuel 17:47.

During the days Saul was king of Israel, a big family lived in the little town of Bethlehem. There were eight brothers and two sisters in the family. The father was an old man named Jesse who must have loved to tell his children stories of their grandfather, Obed; stories of their famous great-grandparents, Ruth and Boaz; and stories of their great-great-grandmother, Rahab, who helped the two spies escape from Jericho.

The three oldest sons of Jesse were brave young men who served in Saul's army. The youngest son took care of his father's sheep. His name was David. He was a strong young man, and people trusted him. He was brave and handsome and deeply tanned from all the hours out in the sun. He also was a fine musician and could play the harp as well as anyone in the country.

A Giant Scare for Israel

But all was not well in Bethlehem. The three oldest sons of Jesse had bad news. Israel was at war again. Their old enemies, the Philistines, were camped not too far away on a hillside in the Valley of Elah, and they were getting ready to launch an attack. So King Saul and his army marched to the valley and camped on a hillside across from the Philistines.

For 40 days the two armies got ready for battle. Every morning the soldiers from each side would run down to the battle lines, shouting war cries and waving their swords.

Suddenly one morning, from the middle of the Philistine mob, a huge, huge man stumbled forward. This man was a giant. He was bigger than the tallest man in the army. Bigger than anyone you've ever seen. The Philistine giant was more than nine feet tall! He wore heavy armor from his neck to his feet. His spear looked like the trunk of a tree. His sword was as tall as any of the Israelite soldiers.

"My name is Goliath," the giant yelled. "I'm the meanest man in the Philistine army. Who wants to fight? Come on."

Of course none of King Saul's soldiers wanted to fight him. Goliath yelled again. "I'll make you a deal. If one of your soldiers can beat me, we'll all become your servants."

The Philistine soldiers laughed at such a thought.

"What's the matter?" shouted Goliath. "Isn't your God strong enough to help you? Isn't He a very good fighter? I think your army, your king, and your God are worthless!"

David Joins the Army

Back in Bethlehem the news was all about the battle soon to be fought in the Valley of Elah. Every day Jesse wondered about his three oldest sons. He was worried that they would be hurt in the battle. Every day the brothers and sisters wondered if they'd ever see their big brothers again.

"I want you to go visit your brothers," Jesse told David one afternoon. "Take them some home-cooked food. Tell them hello for us. Find out if they're safe."

So the next day, early in the morning, David left the sheep he cared for and began walking to the west, straight toward the Valley of Elah. He reached the soldiers' camp just as each army was gathering on their side of the riverbed. David left his things with the keeper of supplies and ran to the battle lines. He found his brothers there and had just begun to talk with them when Goliath stomped into view and began yelling more threats.

"Who is this giant?" David asked his brothers.

"His name is Goliath. He's the meanest man in the Philistine army."

"Why doesn't someone fight him?" asked David.

"Because we're all so afraid of him," one brother explained. "King Saul has promised prizes to anyone who will defeat him, but no one wants to try."

"What has the king promised?" David asked.

"The king promised money," his brothers told him. "He also said that the man who fights Goliath and wins can marry one of his daughters. And now he's promising that the hero's family won't ever have to pay taxes! And still no one's brave enough to try. Not even the king will fight the giant."

The Lion, the Bear, and the Giant

David thought of his family back in Bethlehem. He thought of the sheep he had been taking care of. He thought of the dangers he had faced to protect the sheep. Once a lion had attacked, and another time a bear had tried to steal one of his sheep. And then David made a courageous decision. "I will go and fight Goliath," he announced. "The Lord who saved me from the lion and the bear will also save me from this Philistine."

When the king heard that David wanted to fight the giant, he tried to talk him out of it. "You're just a boy," King Saul said to David. "You don't have the experience that Goliath has. You don't know how to fight."

But David was confident. He knew that God would be with him.

"At least wear my armor," the king said. "That will protect you." So David tried on the king's armor, but it was too big and heavy.

"I can't wear this," David told King Saul.

"Then the Lord be with you," Saul said.

When Goliath saw the young man come toward him, he thought it was a joke. He yelled threats at David, trying to frighten him into running away.

But David did not run. "You come against me with a sword and a spear," he said. "But I come against you in the name of the Lord Almighty, the God of Israel. When our battle is over, everyone here will know that God doesn't need weapons to save us. This battle is the Lord's, and He will give us victory over you and your soldiers."

David ran straight at Goliath. In a moment the fight was over. Goliath was no match for the God of the universe.

On the hillside behind David the soldiers of Saul's army raised their arms in victory and shouted, "We won, we won!"

Yet not one of those soldiers had fought in the battle. The soldiers were winners because of grace—because their champion had beaten the champion of the enemy. They weren't saved because of their bravery or their strength. They were saved because, once again, God had saved His people.

David was a stranger to the earth's way of fighting. How can we follow David's example?

Endnotes for Parents

"The Meanest Man in the Army" is found in 1 Samuel 17.

This is a story about ***grace.***

Grace happens when our Champion fights the enemy, defeats the enemy, and then gives us the victory. We can yell, "We won!" all we want, but the truth is that while we do a lot of shouting we actually don't raise a finger, shoot an arrow, or even draw our swords in the battle for salvation. The victory is *given* to us.

Grace isn't about the prizes that need to be offered to induce us to fight. Nor is ***grace*** about fitting into someone else's armor and fighting the way they have fought. ***Grace*** accepts human weakness in this matter, relying instead on our Champion to wade into the dry riverbed of the salvation battlefield and defeat the giant of sin.

"I will show love to Judah; and I will save them—not by bow, sword or battle, or by horses and horsemen, but I, the Lord their God, will save them" (Hosea 1:7).

"Be strong and courageous. Do not be afraid or discouraged because of the king of Assyria and the vast army with him, for there is a greater power with us than with him. With him is only the arm of flesh, but with us is the Lord our God to help us and to fight our battles" (2 Chron. 32:7, 8).

"Our struggle is not against flesh and blood, but against the rulers, against the authorities, against the powers of this dark world and against the spiritual forces of evil in the heavenly realms. . . . Stand firm then, with the belt of truth buckled around your waist, with the breastplate of righteousness in place, and with your feet fitted with the readiness that comes from the gospel of peace. In addition to all this, take up the shield of faith, with which you can extinguish all the flaming arrows of the evil one. Take the helmet of salvation and the sword of the Spirit, which is the word of God" (Eph. 6:12-17).

A. Skib

10

Good News for Mephibosheth

"Don't be afraid, . . . for I will surely show you kindness."

2 Samuel 9:7.

We all act differently when we hear bad news. Some people cry about bad news. Some people get mad. Some become discouraged. Some people decide to quit listening to the news altogether! How do the people in your family react to bad news?

One day the bad news came that King Saul and his son Jonathan had died.[1] In Jonathan's home, the nurse heard the bad news first. She was taking care of Jonathan's only son, who was 5 years old. His name was Mephibosheth (meh-FIB-oh-sheth). When the nurse heard the news, she picked up the little boy and ran.[2]

But something awful happened. Little Mephibosheth slipped out of the nurse's arms. Maybe she tripped over a toy on the floor. Maybe she slipped in a puddle of water. Or maybe Mephibosheth was wiggly and too heavy to hold. We don't know what caused the accident, but Mephibosheth fell hard to the ground and began to cry.

By the time the nurse got him to a friend's house, his feet were badly swollen. The doctors came and did their best. But nothing helped. He must have broken some bones, because both of Mephibosheth's feet became crippled. He couldn't walk well after that. He couldn't run with the other children. He couldn't even stand up straight. For the rest of his life, when people said his name, they added, "the boy who is crippled in both feet."[3]

Loyal servants of Saul and Jonathan took care of Mephibosheth as best they could. They watched over him. They fed him. One of the servants, Makir, from the town of Lo Debar, took Mephibosheth into his own home and raised him just like one of his own children.

David Asks Questions

One morning, many years later, King David was wondering if any of Saul's relatives were still alive. He thought about how kind his dear friend Jonathan had been to him. *Is there any way I can pay back that kindness?* he wondered. David did not know about Mephibosheth. He had no idea his friend's son was alive. King David had not heard about the accident. He didn't know about Mephibosheth's crippled feet.

But David did remember one of Jonathan's servants, a man named Ziba. He sent soldiers to look for Ziba, and they found him! Ziba now had 15 sons and 20 servants of his own. They all lived quietly, away from Jerusalem, where no one would bother them. Now David's soldiers brought Ziba to the palace. He came before the king and bowed low.

"Are you Ziba?" King David asked.

"At your service," Ziba answered.

David came quickly to the point. "Is anyone from Saul's family still alive?" he asked. "I would like to show God's kindness to them."

"There is someone," Ziba replied. "He is Jonathan's son, a young man named Mephibosheth, who is crippled in both feet."

"Where is he?" David was beginning to get excited.

Ziba told the king how to find Mephibosheth, and David sent soldiers to Lo Debar to bring him to Jerusalem.

A Royal Welcome

Mephibosheth shuffled into the throne room and bowed before the king. David stood up and walked toward this long-forgotten son of his good friend Jonathan.

"Are you Mephibosheth?" David asked gently.

"At your service," Mephibosheth answered. He felt worried. He didn't know why the king wanted him in Jerusalem. Would King David throw him in jail because his grandfather once was David's enemy?

"Don't be afraid, Mephibosheth," David told him. "I will show you kindness because of your father, Jonathan."

Mephibosheth looked up into the king's eyes. He could tell that David was a kind man. Did he really mean it when he said, "Don't be afraid"?

From that day forward Mephibosheth's life completely changed. He was welcomed in the palace. He was given new clothes and good things to eat. He would no longer live with his father's servants. He was given a house in Jerusalem so that he could always be close to the king. What's more, David gave Mephibosheth all the land and the houses that had once belonged to his grandfather, King Saul. That land was now his.

"And there's something else," David said to Mephibosheth. "From now on I want you to eat all your meals with me at my table. I want to treat you just like one of my own children. You are now a son of the king."

Mephibosheth bowed before David again. "I don't deserve such treatment," he said. "I'm not an important person. Why should you even notice me?"

But the king insisted! David wanted to be as kind to Mephibosheth as God had been to him.

Next Ziba was brought back to the palace.

"I have given Mephibosheth everything that belonged to Saul and his family," David explained. "Now I want you and your sons and your servants to farm the land for him. Bring in the crops every year. That way your family and Mephibosheth's family will always have what they need."

Mephibosheth and his young son, Mika, moved into their new home. Every day they rode their donkeys together up the hill to the palace to eat with the king. Ziba and his family continued to watch over Mephibosheth at the country home. And every time they had the chance, they also took good care of King David.[4]

That day turned out to be a wonderful day for Mephibosheth. His life had begun with bad news. But now the boy who was crippled in both feet would live every day with good news. Every day for the rest of his life Mephibosheth ate at the table of the king.

What do we find out about living like "a stranger on earth" from the way David treated Mephibosheth?

Endnotes for Parents

"Good News for Mephibosheth" is from 2 Samuel 9.

---

[1] 1 Sam. 31:1-6.
[2] 2 Sam. 4:4.
[3] 2 Sam. 9:3, 13.
[4] 2 Sam. 16:1, 2.

This is a story about ***grace.***

Grace is how God treats people who once were His enemies—as if they were His very best friends.

Grace is the way God invites us to always eat at His table with Him.

Grace is God saying to us, "I'm going to treat you just as if you are one of my own children. You are now a child of the King."

"You are priceless to me. . . . I will bring your people back from the east. I will gather you from the west. I will say to the north, 'Let them go!' And I will say to the south, 'Do not hold them back.' Bring my sons from far away. Bring my daughters from the farthest places on earth. Bring back everyone who belongs to me" (Isa. 43:4-7, NIrV).

"He came to that which was his own, but his own did not receive him. Yet to all who did receive him, to those who believed in his name, he gave the right to become children of God—children born not of natural descent, nor of human decision or a [parent's] will, but born of God" (John 1:11-13).

"See what great love the Father has lavished on us, that we should be called children of God! And that is what we are! The reason the world does not know us is that it did not know him. Dear friends, now we are children of God, and what we will be has not yet been made known. But we know that when Christ appears, we shall be like him, for we shall see him as he is" (1 John 3:1, 2).

A. Skib

11

The Wise Woman and the King

"He [God] devises ways so that a banished person does not remain banished from him."

2 Sam. 14:14.

King David was not in a good mood. He was on his way to his throne room for another day at work. Every day people from all over the kingdom of Israel came to King David and told him their problems. Then he had to figure out exactly what each of those people should do. It was going to be another long, hard day.

What's more, the king was having family troubles. David and his seven wives had 20 children! There were 19 boys and one girl.[1] Plus there were a lot of other children running up and down the hallways of the royal palace. Sometimes the children complained about their food. Sometimes they got sick and needed extra care. Every now and then the children didn't sleep very well. The king always tried to help.

One day David's oldest son, Amnon, was very mean to his sister, Tamar, and hurt her badly. That made her brother Absalom really mad. Absalom was so mad that he picked a fight with Amnon, and in that fight Amnon died.

Now Absalom was in really big trouble, so he ran away, far away. David had taught his children that God's people behave better than that.[2] David had no choice but to say that Absalom was officially *banished.* He could never come home again.

Three years passed. Absalom was still far away. But King David missed him even though he had done something very wrong. With all those family troubles in mind, David walked to his throne room. He was not in a good mood.

Joab Hopes to Help

Someone very close to the king noticed his bad mood. It was David's nephew Joab. Joab's mom, Zeruiah (Zuh-ROO-ee-ah), was King David's sister![3] Joab wondered if there was something he could do to help his uncle. The more he thought about it, the more he wanted to help. So Joab came up with a great idea.

He sent a friend to a nearby village. In the village lived a woman who everyone said was very wise. Joab's friend asked the woman to come to Jerusalem. There Joab explained his plan. He wanted the woman to tell David a story. He told her exactly what to do and what to say. Joab hoped that when David listened to the story, he would think of his own family troubles. No one would have to say anything personal to the king. He hoped David would realize he should let Absalom come back home.

In the Throne Room

It was crowded in the throne room the next morning. Lots of people had come to hear the king's advice. Slowly the wise woman worked her way through the crowd until she stood right in front of the king. She bowed low and said, "Help me, Your Majesty."

People in the room stopped talking to hear the woman speak. David looked directly into her eyes. "What's troubling you?" he asked.

The woman began to tell the story that Joab had made up for her to say. "My husband died," she said. "So now I'm raising our two boys by myself. A couple of days ago the boys got into a fight with each other. One boy hit the other boy. He fell down, hit his head, and died. Now everyone in the family wants the first boy to be punished for what he did. If that happens, I'll be all alone."

King David listened very carefully. For a moment he thought about what the woman had said. Then he announced his decision.

"I'll make a decree that no one is to hurt your son," David said. "Everything will be fine. You can go home now."

People in the room smiled. They were proud of their wise king. They all expected the woman to say thank you and get up and go. But the wise woman knew that something was wrong. David had not made the connection between the woman's story and his own troubles with Absalom. The plan had not yet worked. The woman thought quickly and then spoke up.

"Excuse me, Your Majesty."

The other people in the room were surprised that the woman kept talking. When the king dismisses you, you should leave! *What does she want now?* they wondered.

"I don't mean to make trouble for you," the woman told King David. "But when my family hears your decision, I'm worried what they will say. I don't want them to blame you."

David replied patiently, "If anyone says anything to you, just bring them to me. They won't bother you again."

The king dismissed her again. But still he didn't get it. Now what should she do?

"Would you be willing to make this a religious decision?" the woman asked. Several people in the room gasped. The woman dared to keep talking! "Would you also ask God to bless us? That will keep anyone in my family from doing anything to my son."

King David rose to his feet. He felt his temper rising. But he controlled himself.

"Yes," he answered calmly. "I'll make my decision even stronger. As surely as the Lord lives, not even one hair of your son's head will be harmed."

That settles that, the people thought. *Our king really handled that well, didn't he?* But wait! The woman was still there. Again she didn't leave. She knew now that Joab's plan was not going to work. She had to say more.

"May I say one more thing to the king?" she asked.

"Speak!" David thundered.

"If you feel so strongly about protecting my son, why have you done such a horrible thing to your own son?"[4]

The woman's voice was strong and clear. No one in the room was making any noise now. All eyes looked at her. Would the king punish her for criticizing him?

"When you announced your decision on my case," the woman said, "you announced your own guilt. You have not brought back your banished son. And let me remind you [she was getting bolder with each sentence], you're not acting like *God*, either. God doesn't kill people. Instead, He figures out a way to bring banished people home!"

David stood with both hands on his hips. He moved slowly toward the woman. She shuddered. Nobody was breathing. You could hear a pin drop in the throne room.

"Now let me ask *you* a question," King David said. Then, after a long pause, his voice softened. "Did Joab have anything to do with this?"

Way over on the side of the room Joab's eyes got very big. *How did David figure it out?* he wondered. *Now what will happen to me?*

Joab walked slowly toward the throne. He bowed low in front of the king and held his breath. David stared down at his nephew. A big frown crossed David's forehead. He sighed.

David Starts to Smile

"I think you made your point," David said, beginning to smile. His smile surprised everyone in the room. "Go get Absalom," he commanded Joab, "and bring him home."

Since the story is about humans, it took a little while to finish. But finally one day Absalom bowed low before his father, the king. David reached down and helped his son to his feet. He looked into Absalom's eyes, then gave his son a big kiss. It was good to have Absalom home. For a little while all of David's family troubles seemed to be over.

By his kind forgiveness of Absalom, David demonstrated that he was "a stranger on earth." How does what you do every day show that you are "a stranger on earth"?

Endnotes for Parents

"The Wise Woman and the King" is taken from 2 Samuel 13 and 14.

---

[1] 1 Chron. 3:1-9.

[2] 2 Sam. 13:12.

[3] 1 Chron. 2:16.

[4] In this story the woman uses a very powerful word. She says, "Why have you *devised* a thing like this against the people of God?" (2 Sam 14:13). In the Bible the word "devise" always is used in the negative: Haman's "evil scheme" (Esther 9:25), the "evil plots" and "wicked schemes" of God's enemies (Ps. 21:11), "false accusations" (Ps. 35:20), "injustice" (Ps. 58:2), "wicked plans" (Nahum 1:11), even the lies the chief priests told the soldiers to tell about what had happened to the body of Jesus (Matt. 28:12).

This strong word has a horrible connotation, with just one exception. The woman also says that God *devises* "ways so that a banished person does not remain banished from him" (2 Sam. 14:14). The wise woman knew that God's love knows how to take even the worst of circumstances and turn them into good.

This is a story about ***grace.***

Grace is the "kiss of the king," which God gives to all of us who have sinned and not behaved like children of King Jesus (Rom. 3:23).

Grace is God going to work to figure out ways He can bring us back to His side. Sin has caused God to banish us all (Gen. 3:23). But ***grace*** means that God also takes the responsibility for ending our estrangement from Him (Jer. 29:13, 14).

"God will restore your fortunes and have compassion on you and gather you again from all the nations where he scattered you. Even if you have been banished to the most distant land under the heavens, from there the Lord your God will gather you and bring you back" (Deut. 30:3, 4).

A. Skib

12

Don't Light the Fire!

"You, Lord, are God, and . . . you are turning their hearts back again."

1 Kings 18:37.

Ahab and Jezebel were the most feared king and queen in all the history of Israel. King Ahab was more wicked than any of the kings before him. Queen Jezebel was worse than any queen Israel had ever seen.[1]

Not only did King Ahab and Queen Jezebel treat their people badly, they also rebelled against God. Ahab set up idols in the places the Israelites worshipped. The king and queen ordered all the prophets of God to be killed.[2] Then they ordered new priests of Baal to take charge of worship.

It was a very unhappy time in Israel. The people were afraid of their king and queen. The prophets of God were hiding in caves. The new priests were mean.

And then, on top of everything else, the rains stopped coming. Without rain, the rivers stopped flowing. The wells dried up. The trees and shrubs turned brown and died. The people began to wonder if they'd ever again have enough water to drink.[3]

Time for a Change

One day God told the prophet Elijah that the people had suffered long enough because of King Ahab and Queen Jezebel. So Elijah arranged a meeting with the king. Ahab was rude as he greeted Elijah. But Elijah came right to the point of the meeting.

"You have made trouble for Israel," Elijah said.

"You have quit praising the God of heaven. The time has come to put an end to the worship of Baal."

"Do you think you can stop 450 prophets of Baal?" Ahab said.

"You bring your prophets to Mount Carmel," Elijah answered. "And invite all the people in Israel to meet us there. We'll see who really is God."

450 Against One

King Ahab did what Elijah suggested. He sent word throughout all the country for the people to meet at Mount Carmel. When everyone was there, Elijah spoke to them.

"How long are you going to go back and forth between two different beliefs?" Elijah asked the people. "If the Lord is God, then you should follow the Lord. But if Baal is god, then follow him. You have to make up your minds."

But the people were afraid. They didn't say anything.

So Elijah decided to show them that the 450 prophets of Baal were leading them in the wrong direction. He wanted them to know that only God in heaven could save them.

"Look," Elijah said, "there are 450 prophets of Baal here, and I'm the only prophet of God. Go get two bulls we can use for sacrifice. We'll let the prophets of Baal choose the best bull for themselves and prepare it to sacrifice. Then I'll prepare the other bull. But we won't light the fire for the burnt offering. Only God will light the fire."

Then Elijah turned to the 450 prophets of Baal.

"When your sacrifice is ready," Elijah told them, "you pray to your god to send down fire. When my sacrifice is ready, I'll pray to my God. But neither one of us can light the fire. We'll leave that to God. The god who answers by sending fire to burn the sacrifice is truly God. Do you agree?"

The 450 prophets of Baal looked fearfully at one another. What else could they do but agree?

Shout Louder

As soon as the bull was ready for sacrifice, the prophets of Baal began praying to their god. At first they prayed quietly. Then they began to shout. Then they danced around the altar they had made. But no fire came out of heaven.

"Baal, answer us," they shouted again and again and again. They made a lot of noise because there were 450 of them! The sun rose high in the sky, and still they shouted. Now it was noon.

"Why don't you shout louder?" Elijah told them. "Maybe your god is busy or away on a trip. Maybe he's sound asleep!"

The 450 prophets of Baal realized they were running out of time. They shouted even louder and danced even faster and prayed even harder. When their time was almost up, they even took out their knives and cut themselves. *Maybe Baal wants our blood*, they thought. But still no fire came out of heaven.

Too Wet to Burn

Now it was evening. The sun began to set over the Mediterranean Sea. The cool breezes began to blow. Elijah called all the people to come around him. He repaired the altar of God that lay in ruins on the mountaintop. He quietly placed the wood on the altar and put the bull on the wood.

Then Elijah did something no one had ever done before. He dug a large ditch around the altar and told the people to fill the ditch with water. It took four large barrels of water to fill the ditch.

"Do it again," Elijah ordered. Again the people brought four barrels of water. They poured the water over the sacrifice. The water covered the wood and ran down the stones of the altar.

"Do it a third time," Elijah ordered. Once more the people brought barrels of water and poured it over the sacrifice, the wood, and the altar.

The people watched Elijah closely. The 450 prophets of Baal watched Elijah. Wicked King Ahab watched Elijah. With all the water drowning the sacrifice, no one could accuse Elijah of playing a trick and lighting the fire himself.

"God doesn't need to be impressed with our efforts" Elijah seemed to be saying. "He doesn't need to be awakened. He doesn't need for us to shout or dance or cut ourselves to get His attention. He doesn't need us to light the fire for Him.

"There is nothing we can do to make God love us more than He already does. He is here this evening, showing us His grace, turning our hearts back to Him again."

Suddenly the evening sky exploded. A bolt of heavenly fire tore through the clouds and shot down on the sacrifice. The fire burned up the sacrifice. It burned up the wood. It burned up all the stones in the altar. It dried up all the water in the ditch. It even burned the ground. Nothing was left. Not a twig. Not a pebble. Not a drop of water.

The people fell to their knees. "The Lord, He is God," they all shouted.

The worship of the God of heaven returned to Israel.

And the rain began to fall again.

Where could you be "a stranger on earth" this week as Elijah was a long time ago on Mount Carmel?

Endnotes for Parents

"Don't Light the Fire!" comes from 1 Kings 18:15-39.

---

[1] 1 Kings 16:29-33.
[2] 1 Kings 18:4.
[3] 1 Kings 17:1-7.

This is a story about ***grace.***

Grace is what gives us peace while we live here in this often unhappy, fearful, dried-up, enemy-held territory called Planet Earth.

Grace is what keeps us worshipping the God of heaven when so many opinions seem to be tempting us to worship worthless idols; when 450 other voices try to entice us to abandon God.

Grace comes to us when we're exhausted from shouting and dancing and cutting ourselves in an attempt to win God's favor. ***Grace*** reminds us that nothing we can do can make God love us more than He already does. ***Grace*** helps us remember that the sacrifice that assures salvation is not kindled with any human fire.

Grace tells us that God is already with us, turning our hearts back to Him again.

"Does the Lord delight in burnt offerings and sacrifices as much as in obeying the Lord? To obey is better than sacrifice, and to heed is better than the fat of rams. For rebellion is like the sin of divination, and arrogance like the evil of idolatry" (1 Sam. 15:22, 23).

"Create in me a pure heart, O God, and renew a steadfast spirit within me. Do not cast me from your presence or take your Holy Spirit from me. Restore to me the joy of your salvation and grant me a willing spirit, to sustain me" (Ps. 51:10-12).

"You are the children that God dearly loves. So be just like him. Lead a life of love, just as Christ did. He loved us. He gave himself up for us. He was a sweet-smelling offering and sacrifice to God" (Eph. 5:1, 2, NIrV).

A. Skib

13

You Don't Need to Fight

"Give thanks to the Lord, for he is good; his love endures forever."

Psalm 106:1.

What would you call someone whose great-great-grandfather was a man named Israel? The Jews would have called him an *Israelite*. Israel's original name was Jacob, but God changed his name to Israel.[1] After that, all of Israel's family members were known as the children of Israel, or simply as Israelites.

If a friend of yours came from the family of Israel's oldest son, Reuben, your friend would be known as a *Reubenite*. If your friend had Israel and Leah's son Levi as their ancestor, they would be called a *Levite*. If your friend came from Gad's family, they would be a *Gadite*.

Who do you think was the ancestor of the *Danite* people? That's right! The man's name must have been Dan. And how about the *Benjamites*? They came from Israel and Rachel's son Benjamin.[2] What would the Jews call the people of your family?

The Jews referred to their neighbors the same way. The Moabites had come from a man named Moab. Ammonites descended from Ben-Ammi.[3] If the neighbors lived in the land of Canaan, the Jews called them *Canaanites*. If the neighbors were from Midian, the Jews knew them as *Midianites*. The *Cushites* were from the land of Cush.

So there were a lot of "*ites*" in Bible times. When a wedding took place, it was one ite marrying another ite. When a treaty was signed, one ite signed for one country and another ite signed for

the other country. If there was a battle, it was one ite fighting against another ite.

At War Again

Now the kingdom of Judah was being attacked again! This time it was the *Moabites* and the *Ammonites* who started the fight. The large enemy army marched from their homes and camped near En Gedi, just west of the Dead Sea.

Up in Jerusalem the people heard the news of the big enemy army. Good King Jehoshaphat[4] called all the people together. They came from all around the country. Jehoshaphat met them at the front of the Temple courtyard. He asked the people to kneel with him and pray for protection.

"Lord, God of our ancestors," the king prayed, "You are the God of heaven. You have been with us ever since You rescued us from Egypt. Even before that, You made promises to our father Abraham, Your dear friend. We have often stood here to worship You at this Temple. We have come to You many times in distress. Now we come again, and we need You to save us."

Then Jehoshaphat did something very important. In front of all the people, he admitted that his large, experienced army[5] was not going to win this fight. They would not be successful if they fought their enemies all by themselves.

"We have no power against this huge army that is attacking us," the king said. "We don't even know what to do. But we're keeping our eyes on You. We know You'll show us what to do." (The king was a *Humble-ite.*)

A Sudden Interruption

Suddenly there was movement in the crowd. A man was pushing and shoving his way through the people. The king's guards reached for their swords and rushed toward the ruckus. Perhaps they thought the man was going to attack their king.

When the guards surrounded the man, he yelled out his name. "I am Jahaziel (Juh-HAY-zee-el)," the man said. "I am a *Levite*, a priest. I have a message that God has given me to tell to the king."

"Let him speak," King Jehoshaphat commanded.

The soldiers brought Jahaziel to the king. He turned to the crowd and spoke loudly. Everyone could hear him.

"Listen to me, King Jehoshaphat and all of you who live in Judah and Jerusalem." The prophet's voice rang through the Temple courtyard. "This is what the Lord says to you: 'Do not be afraid. Do not be discouraged because of this huge army that has come against you. This battle is not your battle. It is God's battle!' "

Then Jahaziel told the people what God wanted them to do. "Tomorrow, march out of Jerusalem. Meet the enemy in the desert by the Dead Sea. But you will not have to fight. Take up your positions. Stand at attention. And watch the Lord save you."

Jehoshaphat and all the people fell to their knees to thank God. Other *Levites* ran to the front of the crowd. Some of them were *Kohathites* and *Korahites*. All the priests began to lead the people in singing. Together they praised God with very loud voices. Their worship was cheerful and noisy. The promise of Jahaziel made the people happy all the way back to their homes. (That day they all were *Joyfulites!*)

The Choir Leads the Battle

Early the next morning the people came together again. King Jehoshaphat greeted as many of his people as he could.

"Have faith in God," the king told them. "Believe what the prophet has told us."

Then the king stopped the soldiers who were ready to march. He surprised the people by announcing an unusual decision.

"Since we are not supposed to fight in this

battle," King Jehoshaphat reminded them, "I want to rearrange the marching order. Today I want the Temple choir to go first. When they reach the hill overlooking the desert and see the enemy army, I want them to start singing."

"What song should we sing?" a choir member called out.

"Sing, 'Give thanks to the Lord, for His love endures forever,'" the king answered.

The choir members all nodded. That was one of their favorite songs. They knew it well and could sing it by heart. People playing trumpets and harps would accompany them.

A couple of hours later, at just the right moment, the choir began to sing. Their voices were strong, and the song was powerful. Out in the desert the enemy soldiers were just waking up. When they heard the choir singing, the enemy became confused. *Maybe the army of Judah has gotten help from somewhere,* they must have thought. *Maybe there are now more of them than there are of us.*

"I'm not going to fight those people," one enemy soldier must have said. He picked up his sleeping bag and began to run away. Others followed him quickly. Soon all the soldiers were tripping over each other as they ran as fast as they could to get away. They raced this way and that. They even started fighting one another as they tried to escape.

Up on the hill the choir kept singing. The soldiers of Jehoshaphat's army stood still and watched what was happening. Just as Jahaziel had promised, they didn't need to fight the battle at all. A great victory happened that day without one single soldier doing any fighting. Judah did indeed have extra help from somewhere else.

It was God who had given them the victory.

How does King Jehoshaphat's choir remind us that we really are "strangers on earth" (*stranger-ites*!)?

Endnotes for Parents

"You Don't Need to Fight" comes from 2 Chronicles 20.

---

[1] Gen. 32:28.

[2] You can check out many of these names in Joshua 13 and Judges 1.

[3] Gen. 19:37.

[4] 2 Chron. 17:3-6; 19:4-11.

[5] 2 Chron. 17:12-19.

This is a story about ***grace.***

Grace reminds us that in the battle for our salvation, even though we face a vast army, we don't need to be afraid or discouraged, for the battle is not ours, but God's.

Grace comes to us whenever we are in distress about whether or not we'll get to heaven. We accept God's ***grace*** as we realize that, when it comes to salvation, we don't even know what to do. Our role is to stand still and keep our eyes on Jesus.

Grace makes us sing, "Give thanks to the Lord, for He is good. His love endures forever."

"Do not be terrified; do not be afraid of them. The Lord your God, who is going before you, will fight for you, as he did for you in Egypt, before your very eyes, and in the wilderness. There you saw how the Lord your God carried you, as a father carries his son, all the way you went until you reached this place" (Deut. 1:29-31).

"You may live a life worthy of the Lord and please him in every way: bearing fruit in every good work, growing in the knowledge of God, being strengthened with all power according to his glorious might so that you may have great endurance and patience, and giving joyful thanks to the Father, who has qualified you to share in the inheritance of his holy people in the kingdom of light. For he has rescued us from the dominion of darkness and brought us into the kingdom of the Son he loves, in whom we have redemption, the forgiveness of sins" (Col. 1:10-14).

A.Skib

14

Open Eyes, Shut Eyes

"There are more on our side than on their side."

2 Kings 6:16, Message.

Elisha the prophet lived in Dothan during the time when a group of people called the Arameans were at war with Israel. They came from the country of Aram. The king of Aram wanted nothing more than to capture the king of Israel and prove that his country was the best.

But the Arameans didn't know Elisha. And they didn't know Elisha's God.

Surprise Attacks

In the war room at the palace where the king of Aram lived, the generals of the Aramean army planned their battle strategy.

"We should attack Israel at Jezreel," said one general.

"That's a good idea," the other generals agreed. "Let's plan a surprise attack at Jezreel."

But down in Dothan God spoke to Elisha.

"Go to the king of Israel," God said to Elisha, "and tell him that the Arameans are going to attack at Jezreel."

Obediently Elisha went to the king and gave him the warning. The king sent his army to Jezreel. When the Arameans arrived for their surprise attack, the army of Israel was ready for them. The Arameans were the ones who were surprised.

"Those lucky Israelites," the Aramean generals said. "How did they just happen to be at Jezreel when we wanted to attack? Let's attack Israel at Beth Shean instead."

"That's a better idea," the other generals agreed. "Let's plan a surprise attack at Beth Shean."

But down in Dothan God spoke to Elisha again.

"Go to the king of Israel," God said, "and let him know that the Arameans are going to attack at Beth Shean."

Elisha went to the king again and gave him the warning. The king sent his army to Beth Shean. When the Arameans arrived for their surprise attack, the army of Israel was ready for them again.

"Those lucky Israelites," the Aramean generals said again. "How did they guess where we were going to attack? Maybe it would be better if we came at them from the east and attacked them at Shechem."

"That's an even better idea," the others agreed. "Let's plan a surprise attack at Shechem."

But down in Dothan, who do you think spoke to Elisha again? That's right!

And what do you suppose God told Elisha? You're right again!

When Elisha told the king of Israel that the Arameans were going to attack at Shechem, where do you think the king sent his army? That's right. Straight to Shechem!

So when the army of the Arameans arrived for their surprise attack at Shechem, who do you think was surprised? Of course!

This time no one said, "Those lucky Israelites!" Instead they said, "How did the Israelites know where we were going to attack *three times in a row*? Someone from our army must have told them!"

Searching for a Traitor

The king of Aram was really mad.

"There's a traitor among us," the king shouted angrily. "Which of you generals is giving our secrets to the king of Israel?"

The Aramean generals trembled in front of their king. "It's not me," said one of the generals. "I'm on your side."

"Not me," said another. "I hate the Israelites."

"Not me," said general number three, "but I know who it is."

The king and all the generals looked at the general who had spoken.

"Tell us who the traitor is," the king demanded. "Which one of you is telling our secrets?"

"It's none of us," general number three answered. "But down in Dothan there's a prophet who speaks for Israel's God. His name is Elisha, and he's the one who's telling our secrets."

"Then go to Dothan and get this Elisha!" the king roared.

So general number three rounded up lots of soldiers and chariots. That night the Arameans rode to Dothan and surrounded the city with their soldiers and chariots and horses. They were ready to capture Elisha.

The Chariots of Fire

The next morning, down in Dothan, Elisha woke up early and went out for his daily walk around the outside of the city. Following quickly behind Elisha was his servant, the man who worked for Elisha every day. But Elisha's servant wasn't watching where he was going. He was looking up into the hillsides around the city. And what he saw scared him.

"Elisha!" the servant shouted. "Look at the soldiers and the chariots surrounding the city. The Arameans are here!"

"Don't be afraid," Elisha told him. "There are more soldiers and chariots on our side than on their side."

Elisha's servant looked around. He didn't see any soldiers from the army of Israel. He didn't see any Israelite chariots. What was Elisha talking about?

Then Elisha prayed to God. "Please open

my servant's eyes," Elisha asked, "so that he can truly see."

God answered Elisha's prayer. Suddenly the servant saw something he had never seen before. He saw thousands of angels from heaven. The angels were riding in chariots of fire. They were ready to save him and his master.

Then Elisha prayed again. "Please, God, close the eyes of our enemies."

Once again God answered Elisha. The soldiers from Aram suddenly became blind. They began to stumble and fall trying to find their way.

Elisha fearlessly walked right up to the Arameans.

"What are you doing here in Dothan?" he asked them. "Let me lead you to Samaria so you can meet the king of Israel."

The soldiers followed Elisha all the way to Israel's capital city. As soon as they were inside the city walls, Elisha asked God to open their eyes again. The soldiers must have been terribly afraid. They were sure their enemy, the Israelites, would want to hurt them.

But the Israelites treated them well. They fed the enemy soldiers a great feast and sent them home.

The Aramean soldiers knew they didn't deserve to be treated so kindly. On the way home they made an important decision.

"If that's the kind of God that Israel serves, we must stop fighting Him," they decided. And so it was that the Aramean soldiers never raided Israel's territory again.

Elisha had taught his enemies to see how good God is.

Where do you think Elisha learned how to be "a stranger on earth"?

Endnotes for Parents

"Open Eyes, Shut Eyes"
comes from 2 Kings 6:8-23.

This is a story about ***grace.***

Grace is the startling realization that even though our enemy's forces are many and have come against us, they are no match for God in the salvation battle. God has more angels than anyone can count, and God will use them when we ask for His help. There are more on our side than there are on their side.

Grace opens our eyes to things that Jesus wants us to know. Through the eyes of ***grace*** we see victory while the battle is still raging.

"God's angel sets up a circle of protection around us while we pray. Open your mouth and taste, open your eyes and see—how good God is" (Ps. 34:7, 8, Message).

"I am sending you to them to open their eyes and turn them from darkness to light, and from the power of Satan to God, so that they may receive forgiveness of sins and a place among those who are sanctified by faith in me" (Acts 26:17, 18).

"I counsel you to buy from me gold refined in the fire, so you can become rich; and white clothes to wear, so you can cover your shameful nakedness; and salve to put on your eyes, so you can see" (Rev. 3:18).

A. Skib

15

The King Becomes a Student

"Show me your ways, Lord, teach me your paths."
Psalm 25:4.

Daniel had been going to school in Babylon for three years. He was a very good student. He listened carefully to his teachers. He did well on all his tests. By now he could easily speak the Babylonian language. He also knew the stories the Babylonians loved to tell. King Nebuchadnezzar was quite proud of his young student.

One night the king had a strange dream. In his sleep Nebuchadnezzar saw something that bothered him. He didn't understand it, but he had dreamed about something very, very big. The big thing was shiny and colorful. It was so bright it had almost blinded him. And whatever that big thing was, it had reminded him of something or somebody he knew.

The trouble was that Nebuchadnezzar could not remember his dream. When he woke up he had an uneasy feeling. He tossed and turned in his bed. He got up and walked back and forth in his bedroom. What was that dream? All he could remember was that it had scared him.

Now he was worried and upset. As the night wore on, the king got angrier and angrier.

The King Calls for the Wise Men

By morning King Nebuchadnezzar was furious. He yelled at everyone in the palace. "Bring me all the wise men in Babylon," he roared. "Get them here right now!"

The servants ran quickly out of the room. They told every wise man they could find to hurry to the palace. From every corner of the

city the wise men came running. They ran in before the king and bowed low.

"Tell me what I dreamed last night!" Nebuchadnezzar demanded. "I'm worried about the dream, and I want to know what it means."

"We're so sorry you're upset, Your Majesty," one of the wise men answered. "Just tell us the dream, and we'll tell you what it means."

"I can't remember the dream," the king shouted back. "Why do you think I called all of you here? You tell me what the dream was, and tell me right now, or you'll be sorry you ever lived in Babylon. I'll smash all your houses and turn them into piles of trash. Then I'll do the same to you!"

Suddenly Nebuchadnezzar took a deep breath. He lowered his voice and spoke quietly. "But if you *do* tell me the dream, I'll give you a lot of presents. I'll tell everyone to treat you with respect. You'll be rich and famous. NOW, TELL ME THE DREAM!"

"Please, Your Majesty," another wise man said. "Just let us know what the dream was about and we can explain it to you."

"I can't!" the king shouted. "I don't *remember* the dream! You're just trying to stall for time so you can make something up. You say you're so wise, but you're all liars! Tell me the dream right now, or you'll be sorry."

Another wise man stepped forward and bowed before Nebuchadnezzar. "No king has ever asked his wise men to do such a thing," he pleaded. "No wise man can possibly do what the king asks. Only God could tell you your dream, and He doesn't live here!"

That was the wrong answer! Nebuchadnezzar had never been so mad before. He shouted for the soldiers. "Arrest them all," he roared. "Take them to prison until I write up a decree. I'll have you punish every wise man in Babylon."

Daniel Asks for Help

A few minutes later the king's head soldier, a man named Arioch, pushed open Daniel's door. "You're in big trouble," Arioch told Daniel. "The king is going to punish all the wise men in the country."

"Why is the king doing such an awful thing?" Daniel asked.

Arioch told Daniel that the king had dreamed a bad dream, but he couldn't remember what it was, and the wise men couldn't help him.

Daniel knew that this was a problem for God, so he asked Arioch to give him one day to pray. "Then I'll tell the king his dream," he promised.

Arioch agreed.

Daniel and his three best friends met in Daniel's house. They talked about what Nebuchadnezzar wanted. Then they asked the God of heaven to help them. "The king's dream is a mystery to us," they prayed. "We don't know what it is or what it means. Please show us the answer to this mystery."

When Daniel woke up the next morning, he knew that God had answered his prayer. The mystery was solved. Daniel knew what he would tell the king.

"Thank You, God," he prayed. "You are the one who gives wisdom. You show us mysterious and hidden things. You know our deep, dark secrets and bring them out into the light."

Daniel Explains the Dream

Arioch marched Daniel into the king's palace. "I have found a young man from Judah," Arioch said. "He will tell the king what his dream means."

Nebuchadnezzar was very interested. But Daniel didn't call attention to himself. "There is a God in heaven," Daniel said, "and He's the one who solves mysteries. This is what God has shown me.

"In your dream you saw a large, bright statue of a man. The statue's head was made from pure gold. Its chest and arms were made of shiny silver. Its stomach and thighs were made from beautiful bronze. The statue had strong legs of iron. And its feet were a mixture of iron and clay."

"That's right!" Nebuchadnezzar shouted. "That's exactly what I saw."

"But there's more," Daniel told him. "In your dream you saw a rock being cut from a mountain. But there were no workers cutting the rock. No one on earth was helping to make it. You saw the rock fly through the air and smash into the statue. The beautiful, bright statue of a man toppled over and broke into pieces."

"That's it!" Nebuchadnezzar repeated. "You've got it. You know my dream. Now tell me what it means."

"Your Majesty," Daniel began, "you are the head of gold. You are the mighty king of this powerful kingdom. But one day another kingdom will follow you. It won't be as strong as yours, but it also will rule the earth. Then another kingdom will come, a third one. And then another and another. Each of the kingdoms will do all they can to show how strong they are. They'll do everything possible to hold on to their power. But each one of them will fail and be defeated by the next kingdom.

"But then God's kingdom will take over. The rock represents God's kingdom. It will replace all the kingdoms here on earth. It will grow and grow until it fills the whole world. No other kingdom will come after it. No other kingdom will destroy it. God's kingdom will last forever."

Nebuchadnezzar sat silently in front of Daniel. Then he fell down on his knees to show his humble attitude. "Your God is the greatest god of all," he said to Daniel. "He even rules over kings like me! He teaches us the answers to mysteries. I will try to be His good student."

How did Daniel show King Nebuchadnezzar how important it is to be "a stranger on earth"?

Endnotes for Parents

"The King Becomes a Student" is based on Nebuchadnezzar's dream recorded in Daniel 2.

This is a story about ***grace.***

Grace reminds us that no matter how hard we try to dazzle the world with our beauty or intimidate the world with our power, all of that will come crashing down in the presence of God's kingdom.

Grace teaches us that what really lasts is the kingdom of God. That kingdom is cut out "without hands," with no help from us. God's kingdom is God's creation. We can call attention to it. But we don't form it by the things we do.

God's kingdom of ***grace*** lasts forever.

"In my vision at night I looked, and there before me was one like a son of man, coming with the clouds of heaven. He approached the Ancient of Days and was led into his presence. He was given authority, glory and sovereign power; all nations and peoples of every language worshiped him. His dominion is an everlasting dominion that will not pass away, and his kingdom is one that will never be destroyed" (Dan. 7:13, 14).

"Grace and peace to you from him who is, and who was, and who is to come, and from the seven spirits before his throne, and from Jesus Christ, who is the faithful witness, the firstborn from the dead, and the ruler of the kings of the earth. To him who loves us and has freed us from our sins by his blood, and has made us to be a kingdom and priests to serve his God and Father—to him be glory and power for ever and ever! Amen" (Rev. 1:4-6).

Scripture Index